STOOGISM
Anthology

edited by Paul F. Fericano

Scarecrow Books

ACKNOWLEDGMENTS:

Photo Credits: Columbia Pictures, Ludlow Sales and Roger W. Langton (for his crazy Wednesday night photo extravaganza).

Article Credit: Leonard Maltin's article, "The Three Stooges," taken from *The Great Movie Shorts* by Leonard Maltin. Copyright 1972 by Leonard Maltin. Used by permission of Crown Publishers, Inc.

My thanks to the following people for the information and support they provided: Joe Besser, Paul Freeman, Jay Gosney, John Cawley, Jr., Jeff Lenburg, Bob Frischmann, Alan Press, Jeanne Hyun, Beth McNabb, Darla Crockett, Dick Ellington, Marty Gateman, Thomas Silk, and the gang at CROW.

A very special thanks to Edward Bernds for giving more than I had hoped for, to Mike Hawks of *Eddie Brandt's Saturday Matinee* in North Hollywood, to Greg Siliato for buying the two beers that led to all this, and to Katherine, whose support and encouragement made all of this possible. And last, but not *least,* to the Three Stooges themselves for making a great many of us realize the importance of a good pie in the face.

POETRY CREDITS:

"Huck" by Fred Thaballa first appeared in *Speak 2.*

"Robot" by Al Fogel first appeared, in somewhat altered form, in *Oakwood 1.*

"Money Talks" by Art Cuelho first appeared in *Word.*

"Math Problem" by James Magorian is from his book, *Bosnia and Herzegovina* (Third Eye Press).

"Truth" by Terry W. Brown first appeared in the "poets-card" series (#6) from Scarecrow Books.

Steven Ford Brown's poems are from his new book, *George Washington, American Mother, Hollywood Laundromats & The Discovery of Mars.*

"The Sign Said" by Ronald Koertge is from his book, *Men Under Fire* (Duck Down Press).

ISBN: 0-916296-01-6
Library of Congress Catalog Card No.: 77-76619

SCARECROW BOOKS
1050 Magnolia, #2
Millbrae, CA 94030

Table of Contents

Table of Contents (continued):

Introduction

*"We STOOGE together, we STOOGE alone, we
STOOGE when we don't even realize it—and that
is what makes this life interesting."*
—Marty Gateman

In the Thirties and early Forties, theaters were jammed with fans eager to be entertained by the Three Stooges and their special brand of slapstick. Frequently, their 2-reelers were billed as the main attraction, with the feature films offered as an extra dividend. Today the Stooges' wild antics can still be seen on over 160 television stations across the country and all over the world. Their humor has endured.

It is this humor that has not only been enjoyed by people, but also criticized. Concerning the violence often depicted in the Stooges' films, it seems they have been made the scapegoat by many critics who deplore their "acts of destruction." But Stephen Bowles makes an interesting observation in his article on the Stooges (*Films In Review,* Aug./Sept., 1975) when he tells us: "In more recent years . . . few characters have been depicted as so actively violent and methodically self-destructive as the Coyote in the Road Runner cartoons. Yet the violence of Chaplin, Laurel & Hardy, The Marx Brothers, the Coyote and countless others tends to be forgiven while the violence of the Three Stooges is constantly considered a blatantly anti-social behavior model."

Bowles goes on to point out that ". . . it is also to be remembered that the wholesale indulgence in violence by the Stooges is always (like cartoon violence) immediate and harmless. Whether competing with technological or human adversaries, the victims are always momentarily restored to health without physical or emotional damage."

Even the Soviet Union got into the act when they requested some of the Three Stooges' films, and were turned down. It seemed the Soviets' only intentions were to use the films to inaccurately depict "capitalistic violence in America": being kicked in the shins, poked in the eyes and conked over the heads.

Like many actors who use "stand-ins" for more hazardous scenes, the Stooges too had their doubles who at times took their places in front of the camera. They were all talented, skilled stuntmen/actors who did their job well. For years, Johnny Kascier (who was in his 60s), doubled for Curly and later for Moe. Larry was doubled a lot by Teddy Mangean, and Shemp's double was Hurley Breen.

Moe (Harry) Howard was the boss off the screen as well as on. He was an intelligent and warm man to those who knew and worked with him.

Larry Fine was the frizzy-haired Stooge on screen who always seemed to be getting in everyone's way. In some scenes you would see Larry playing the violin, and he was playing it —being an accomplished violinist.

Curly (Jerry) Howard, Moe's younger brother, was the stooge with the shaved head who was given to fits of running in place and uttering his famous "woo-woo-woos." He displayed a marvelous backward child quality that no other comedian has since been able to equal. His spontaneity in most of the Stooges' earlier 2-reelers created for him one of the most absurd characters ever to appear on the screen. When it came time for the right facial expression, Curly was a genius. A serious stroke in 1947, however, forced him to retire. After a long illness, he passed away in 1952 and comedy lost one of its finest clowns.

Shemp (Sam) Howard, Moe and Curly's older brother, rejoined the Stooges in 1947 to take Curly's place. Shemp, who was part of the original trio in vaudeville, was an accomplished actor who had branched out to other areas in the acting world. In character, Shemp immediately created a "stooge" who possessed an almost incredible dumbness. He made his first 2-reeler with the Stooges in a short called *Fright Night,* directed by Edward Bernds.

"Shemp was a delight to work with; a hard worker and a real trouper," recalls Bernds. "He wasn't the same as Curly, perhaps not even as funny as Curly at his best in the old 2-reelers of the '30s, but Shemp was actually a better actor and a more inventive comic. In writing for Shemp, I had the feeling that I was writing for a different character, not just an imitation of Curly."

Sadly enough, Shemp suffered a fatal heart attack in 1955.

He was replaced by veteran comic Joe Besser, who added a new dimension and flavor to the Stooges. He went under his own name and was the last "stooge" to do the 2-reelers with the Stooges when their contract with Columbia expired in 1957.

Because Besser's wife was ailing at the time, he left the trio and was replaced by another accomplished comedian, Joe DeRita. DeRita was a talented burlesque comic and starred, as Curly-Joe, in all the feature films the Stooges made thereafter. The last film they made together was called *Kook's Tour,* which has never been released.

It was during the filming of *Kook's Tour* that Larry suffered a stroke that would leave him partially paralyzed until his death in January of 1975. Moe, who had cancer, passed away only five months later.

The Stooges undoubtedly had something no other comedy team ever had: The ability to bounce back time and time again and transmit their energy to audiences, both old and new, who never seemed to tire of their humor. They held the longest ongoing studio contract in the history of the motion picture business (24 years) and worked together as a team for over 50 years.

A sad truth is that they have been sorely underrated for their comic genius and badly denied any recognition for their unique contribution to comedy in practically every book ever written about Hollywood, motion pictures, comedy teams and even vaudeville.

One of the reasons why you probably don't see a flood of books about this great comedy team, and aren't likely to, is because the name "The Three Stooges" cannot be used in the title of any book without permission from the corporation that owns and carefully protects the special rights to the name.

This anthology is a small, but fond tribute to a very funny team of comics. It does not pretend to be a comprehensive book about the lives of these men, nor does it assume any other function other than providing the reader with a little nostalgia, enjoyment and appreciation for the finer STOOGISM things in life. The poets in this anthology offer their poetry in the same light.

There is STOOGISM in every one of us. Quite simply its philosophy says: Take a good look at life around you, find the laughter, make the very best of living—and then "wake up and go to sleep."

—Paul F. Fericano
Millbrae, California
January 16, 1977

"The Three Stooges"

by Leonard Maltin

In the sound era, no one topped the Three Stooges for longevity and productivity in the two-reeler field. From 1934 to 1958 they starred in 190 comedies for Columbia Pictures; and their shorts continue to be shown today on television stations around the world, capturing the fancy of a whole new generation of fans.

The Stooges' appeal, then and now, is basic. Their humor is built on slapstick and violence, two commodities of universal appeal, and few comics could ever bring off this kind of low comedy as well as the Stooges.

Moe Howard recently explained the formula for their two-reelers: when it came time to fashion a new story, they would think. "Where would we be most out of place?" and on that premise a comedy would be developed. The great part of this was that the Stooges seemed out of place *anywhere,* for their characterizations were, from the very beginning, never quite real.

Moe was, of course, the domineering member of the trio, always barking orders and usually being the butt of their subsequent backfire. Jerry "Curly" Howard (later Sam "Shemp" Howard, still later Joe Besser, and finally Joe DeRita) was the patsy of the group, the fall guy who usually had more going on in his head than anyone would ever suspect. Like Harpo in the Marx Brothers, Curly was slightly surreal, and his bizarre little quirks were never questioned. In *In the Sweet Pie and Pie,* for instance, the threesome are in jail, bemoaning their fate, and Moe mutters, "If we only had some tools." Curly turns to him and asks, "How about these?" He lifts up his shirt and there, tucked into his pants, are a dozen shop utensils of various kinds—saws, files, and so forth. Larry usually got caught in the middle of his two compatriates' schemes, generally going along with the ideas and then sharing in the consequences.

If there is an art to violence, then the Three Stooges were among the few to master it. Over the years they devised seemingly endless variations on ways to slap, poke, and hit one another and somehow make it funny. The trick to the humor was to eliminate the pain; when

1

A scene from *Three Little Pigskins,* 1934, with Phyllis Crane.

this failed, the action would become vulgar instead of funny—a mishap that occurred all too often.

The Stooges' basic formula was developed while they were working with comedian Ted Healy in vaudeville. Healy was a boyhood friend of Moe Howard, and later, when both were working in vaudeville, they teamed up and worked out an act; Moe would heckle Healy from the audience. One day when Moe's older brother, Shemp, was watching the performance, they brought him into the action, and he decided to stay. In 1925, they met Larry Fine, who had been with an odd musical act called Haney Sisters and Fine. From there, Ted Healy and his Stooges (also known as Ted Healy and his Gang, Ted Healy and His Southern Gentlemen, and Ted Healy and his Racketeers) became a staple on the top vaudeville circuits around the country. They played on Broadway, and even did a film in 1930 called *Soup to Nuts.*

When Healy accepted a more substantial offer from MGM several years later, the act had taken on a new member, Moe's younger brother Jerry, who became known as "Curly." Shemp left the act when he got a promising offer from Vitaphone in New York. Curly made an ideal stooge, and the team spent a happy year at

MGM doing small parts in feature films like *Dancing Lady*, with Clark Gable and Joan Crawford, and starring in five two-reelers on their own, some of which were filmed in Technicolor.

There was a young director at MGM during this period who got the chance to start his own comedy department at Columbia in 1934. His name was Jules White. One of the first acts he hired to star in his films was the Three Stooges; their mentor, Ted Healy, remained at MGM. White recalls, "I met the Stooges when we were all at MGM. They were funny, no question about that. Once they were on their own, it didn't take us long to prove it. I made sure they had good material, good directors, good casts."

It took a little while for the Stooges to hit their stride at Columbia, even though their second short, *Men in Black,* was nominated for an Academy Award. They first hit the bull's-eye when they were given a new director, Del Lord. Lord was trained in the Mack Sennett school of comedy, and he was the perfect director for the Stooges; he brought a fast pace and a wealth of gag material with him and, before long, was making a string of hilarious comedies.

Lord took one of his all-time best gags, used in a silent short with Billy Bevan, and gave it to Curly in *Dutiful But Dumb* (1942). Curly is trying to eat a bowl of soup, but instead has to do battle with an ornery clam which is apparently very much alive and determined to turn the soup into a battleground. The clam steals Curly's crackers, squirts him, and in general makes things difficult. As funny as the gag was when Billy Bevan did it, it worked twice as well for Curly, whose portrayal of frustration was unequaled by any other screen comic.

Another good director who worked with the Stooges was Charley Chase. He too had a storehouse of material to draw upon, and made good use of it. A key sequence in *Tassels in the Air* (1938), in which the Stooges try to paint a kitchen table, but paint one another more than anything else, was reworked from Chase's own comedy *Luncheon at Twelve* (1933). Done with a careful, deliberate pacing, the sequence was one of the Stooges' all-time best.

Good directors weren't everything to the Stooges, of course; if the material wasn't there, there was only so much a director could do. Del Lord had his misfires, as did Charley Chase. Lord's *Movie Maniacs* (1935), with the irresistible premise of the Stooges running a movie

3

studio, promised much more than it delivered. *Cash and Carry* (1937) was an oddly sentimental venture for three comics who depended heavily on knockabout farce.

Once they had a good story idea with built-in gags in it, the Stooges were home free; if the director on that particular short knew how to make the most of this material, it turned out even better. Del Lord's *An Ache in Every Stake* (1941), written by veteran comedy director Lloyd French, doesn't have a wasted frame from beginning to end. It opens with the boys as icemen, forced to deliver to a home situated on top of a tremendous flight of steps (not unlike Laurel and Hardy's situation in *The Music Box*). By the time Curly climbs up the steps, his block of ice has melted to the size of an ice cube! The first solution that Moe proposes is to take up *two* blocks of ice, so that, allowing for shrinkage, he will end up with one at the end of his trip. This time, of course, Curly has *two* ice cubes.

After conquering the ice problem, the boys offer their services to the lady of the house as cooks par excellence, to prepare food for her husband's birthday party. This leads into another set of gags in the kitchen, including a wonderful scene in which Curly is told to "shave some ice." He treats the block of ice like a human being and launches into a stream of typical barber patter. Finally, at the party itself, the boys horn in on the guests and generally make a mess of things.

One is left breathless at the end of the short; it moves about as quickly as humanly possible, yet none of the gags seems rushed or abrupt. The continuity flows, and the transitions, from delivering ice to cooking dinner to attending the party, seem perfectly natural—qualities often lacking from the best two-reel comedies.

Director Edward Bernds, who joined the Stooges in 1945, explained how a typical short would come into being. "We'd usually have kind of a bull session in which the boys would wander all over the place, ad-libbing routines, reminiscing, and I would make notes. I would borrow from old scripts too, but mostly I listened. I would stockpile routines, devise some sort of a framework for them to hang onto. I would then write a rough-draft script and call them in. They would go through the first draft; it would give them other notions, and I would make cuts and additions, and somehow hammer out a further draft so that it was pretty much agreed upon by the time it got into final draft."

The Stooges were aided and abetted by a fine group of character comics who comprised a stock company at

Columbia. Either Bud Jamison or Vernon Dent was in every film they made; these veteran actors made every scene count, and their presence was of inestimable value. Symona Boniface, the perfect dowager, was a superb foil for the Stooges in slapstick situations, where she invariably wound up with a pie in the face. Christine McIntyre made dozens of shorts with the team, as either heroine or villainess; as often as possible, it was contrived to make use of her fine singing voice (most notably in the delightful short *Micro-Phonies*). Dorothy Appleby, Emil Sitka, Kenneth MacDonald, Gene Roth, Phil Van Zandt, Gino Corrado, Fred Kelsey, Dick Curtis, and Bruce Bennett were among the many other supporting players who brought their comic know-how to the Stooges' comedies.

In the mid-1940s Curly became very ill. He tried to remain active, but by 1946 it was evident from his screen appearances that he was not well; his actions were slower and his youthful vitality practically gone. He retired in

A scene from *Hoi Polloi,* 1935. The Stooges are failing in their first lesson on how to become "gentlemen."

1946, returning just once to make an amusing cameo appearance in *Hold That Lion* (1947).

The original "third stooge," Shemp, was rerecruited for the trio, and made himself at home quite easily. An undisputably talented comic, Shemp held his own in the Stooges shorts, but he simply could not take the place of Curly, upon whom so much of the comedy depended. When one thinks of the best Three Stooges shorts, almost all of them are those that featured Curly: *Pardon My Scotch, Healthy, Wealthy, and Dumb, In the Sweet Pie and Pie, An Ache in Every Stake, Micro-Phonies, A-Plumbing We Will Go,* and so forth.

Moreover, at the time Shemp joined the Stooges, Columbia was tightening its belt when it came to making the two-reelers. Remakes and stock footage abounded; very elaborate sight gags were pretty much out of the question. The best craftsmen in shorts were no longer active, although some of the younger breed, like Ed Bernds, carried on their tradition. Using every means to overcome budgetary restrictions, Bernds even wrote stories to fit available sets.

He explains, "I recall the day I walked in on Stage 7 at Columbia and saw them building this beautiful castle. I immediately went to Hugh McCollum (the producer) and got an OK to do two stories. I wrote one, *Squareheads of the Round Table,* and Elwood Ullman wrote one called *Hot Scots,* both of them shot on those sets. We started writing the scripts while the sets were being built. We put the scripts aside until the picture (I think it was *Lorna Doone*) was all shot, and then we could use pretty much any set that was still standing."

One of Curly's best shorts, *A-Plumbing We Will Go,* was remade as *Vagabond Loafers,* and turned out to be one of Shemp's best as well. In it, he tries to fix a leaky bathtub by adding one pipe after another, eventually trapping himself inside a maze of metal, the water still shooting out of the open end he has not been able to plug! Not content simply to reshoot this old footage, director Jules White also added a new subplot to the film that enabled him to splice in stock footage of the Stooges' mammoth pie fight from *Half-Wits Holiday* (footage that found its way into innumerable two-reelers). In 1956, the entire film was re-used as *Scheming Schemers.*

From the early 1950s onward, Jules White took over as producer-director of all the Three Stooges shorts. A competent director with plenty of comedy background,

6

White nevertheless did not have the sense of timing many of his colleagues possessed, nor did he have good taste. Sight gags were fewer and the violence greater in his shorts, and, through the 1950s, he missed his mark more often than he hit it.

The Stooges experimented with different kinds of comedy, with varying degrees of success. Some of their shorts tackled political satire, adult situations, and situation comedy, but, oddly enough, only in the first category did the team succeed. The film in question was *Three Dark Horses,* released during the 1952 presidential campaign.

Jules White also experimented wtih the 3-D rage, testing it out on a short called *Spooks* (1953). As comedy it was fair, but the 3-D gimmick turned out to be just that, and White and Columbia decided to drop the whole idea.

In 1955, Shemp Howard died; he was replaced by veteran comic Joe Besser. The shorts that followed are probably the worst comedies the Stooges ever made, but they do have one saving grace—Besser's comedic talent. It was his vitality that gave those two-reelers what life they had. Several of the shorts made liberal use of stock footage, *Pies and Guys* harking back to *Half-Wits Holiday,* and *Rusty Romeos* repeating *Corny Casanovas* from several years before. Some of these shorts were filmed in exactly *one day.* In fact, they were shot so quickly, and so close together, that although the Stooges stopped working for Columbia in January of 1958, the studio had enough material to release new shorts into early 1959.

Since that time, the Stooges have taken on a new partner, Joe DeRita, known as Curly Joe, and have starred in a handful of compactly made feature films and a series of animated cartoons for television. While they received no residuals from the shorts, the constant telecast of the two-reelers on television stations was responsible for returning the Three Stooges to the limelight. It is these comedies, more than anything else, that keep their names alive.

Just as it is impossible for a television series to maintain consistently superior quality on a week-to-week basis, so it was with the prolific Three Stooges. In twenty-four years of two-reelers, they certainly had their ups and downs. But when there was a spark, when a combination of juices flowed from director, writer, cast, and the Stooges themselves, the results were superb. The best of the Three Stooges shorts can hold their own against any other shorts made during Hollywood's golden age of comedy.

7

"The Three Stooges" Shorts

Following is a complete list of the Stooges' starring shorts for Columbia. Prior to these, they appeared with Ted Healy in one of Paramount's "Hollywood on Parade" reels, a "Screen Snapshots," and a handful of shorts for MGM, some of them filmed in color (titles include *Hello Pop, The Big Idea, Beer and Pretzels,* and *Plane Nuts*). Later, they appeared in several other "Screen Snapshots" entries for their home stuido, Columbia, which released all the following two-reelers:

1. *Woman Haters* (5/5/34). Archie Gottler. Marjorie White, A. R. Haysel, Monty Collins, Bud Jamison, Snowflake, Jack Norton, Don Roberts, Tiny Sandford, Dorothy Vernon, Les Goodwin, Charles Richman, George Gray, Gilbert C. Emery, Walter Brennan. The story of three woman haters, with the dialogue spoken in rhyme.

2. *Punch Drunks* (7/13/34). Lou Breslow. Dorothy Granger, Arthur Housman, William Irving, Jack "Tiny" Lipson, Billy Bletcher, Al Hill. Curly gets fighting mad every time he hears "Pop Goes the Weasel."

3. *Men in Black* (9/28/34). Raymond McCarey. Dell Henderson, Jeanie Roberts, Ruth Hiatt, Irene Coleman, Billy Gilbert, Little Billy, Arthur West, Bud Jamison, Hank Mann, Joe Mills, Bob Callahan, Phyllis Crane, Carmen André, Helen Splane, Kay Hughes, Eve Reynolds, Eve Kimberly, Lucile Watson, Billie Stockton, Betty André, Arthur Rankin, Neal Burns, Joe Fine, Charles Dorety, Charles King. Doctors Fine, Howard, and Howard dedicate themselves "to duty and humanity" as they systematically wreck a hospital's decorum. Nominated for an Academy Award.

4. *Three Little Pigskins* (12/8/34). Raymond McCarey. Lucille Ball, Gertie Green, Phyllis Crane, Walter Long, Joseph Young, Milton Douglas, Harry Bowen, Lynton Brent, Bud Jamison, Dutch O. G. Hendrian, Charles Dorety, William Irving, Joe Levine, Alex Hirschfield, Billy Wolfstone, Bobby Burns, Jimmie Phillips, Johnny Kascier. A gambler mistakes the Stooges for three ace football players.

5. *Horses Collars* (1/10/35). Clyde Bruckman. Dorothy Kent, Fred Kohler, Fred Kelsey. The Stooges are sent out West by detective Hyden Seek to help a young girl being victimized by a local villain.

6. *Restless Knights* (2/20/35). Charles Lamont. Geneva Mitchell, Walter Brennan, Chris Franke, George Baxter, James

Howard, Bud O'Neill, Stanley Blystone, Jack Duffy, Ernie Young, Lynton Brent, Bobby Burns, William Irving, Joe Perry, Al Thompson, Bert Young, Dutch Hendrian, George Speer, Billy Franey. To uphold their royal heritage (their father married the royal chambermaid) the Stooges protect their queen.

7. *Pop Goes the Easel* (3/29/35). Del Lord. Leo White, Bobby Burns, Jack Duffy, Elinor Vandivere, Geneva Mitchell (?). The Stooges run amuck in an artists' studio, climaxing in a clay-throwing melee.

8. *Uncivil Warriors* (4/26/35). Del Lord. Theodore Lorch, Lew Davis, Marvin Loback, Billy Engle, Ford West, Si Jenks, Charles Dorety, Jack Kenny, Bud Jamison, Phyllis Crane, Jennifer Gray, Celeste Edwards, Wes Warner, Lew Archer, Hubert Diltz, Charles Cross, George Gray, Jack Rand, Harry Keaton, James C. Morton. The boys are Duck, Dodge, and Hide, Union spies sent to the South to get enemy secrets during the Civil War.

9. *Pardon My Scotch* (8/1/35). Del Lord. Nat Carr, James C. Morton, Billy Gilbert, Grace Goodall. The boys unwittingly become bootleggers.

10. *Hoi Polloi* (8/29/35). Del Lord. Harry Holmes, Robert Graves, Bud Jamison, Grace Goodall, Betty McMahon, Phyllis Crane, Geneva Mitchell, Kathryn Kitty McHugh, James C. Morton, William Irving, Arthur Rankin, Robert McKenzie, Celeste Edwards, Harriett De Bussman, Mary Dees, Blanche Payson, George B. French, Gail Arnold, Don Roberts, Billy Mann. A professor bets a colleague that he can turn the Stooges into gentlemen. Remade as *Half-Wits Holiday* and *Pies and Guys;* stock footage used in *In the Sweet Pie and Pie.*

11. *Three Little Beers* (11/28/35). Del Lord. Bud Jamison. The boys decide to enter a golf tournament sponsored by their beer company.

12. *Ants in the Pantry* (2/6/36). Preston Black (Jack White). Clara Kimball Young, Harrison Green, Bud Jamison, Isabelle LeMal, Vesey O'Davoren, Douglas Gerrard, Anne O'Neal, James C. Morton, Arthur Rowlands, Phyllis Crane, Al Thompson, Helen Martinez, Charles Dorety, Hilda Title, Bert Young, Lew Davis, Ron Wilson, Bobby Burns, Lynton Brent, Arthur Thalasso, Elaine Waters, Althea Henly, Idalyn Dupré, Stella LeSaint, Flo Promise, Gay Waters. The boys are exterminators who create their own business at a swanky party. Remade as *The Pest Man Wins.*

13. *Movie Maniacs* (2/20/36). Del Lord. Bud Jamison, Lois Lindsey, Arthur Henly, Eve Reynolds, Kenneth Harlan, Mildred Harris, Harry Semels, Antrim Short, Jack Kenny, Charles Dorety, Elaine Waters, Bert Young. The Stooges are mistaken for three New York experts who have taken charge of a Hollywood studio.

14. *Half-Shot Shooters* (4/30/36). Preston Black. Stanley Blystone, Vernon Dent, Harry Semels, John Kascier. Even when

they're discharged, the Stooges can't seem to escape their ornery top sergeant.

15. *Disorder in the Court* (5/30/36). Preston Black. Susan Karaan, Dan Brady, Tiny Jones, Bill O'Brien, Bud Jamison, Harry Semels, Edward LeSaint, Hank Bell, James C. Morton. The boys are star witnesses in a murder case.

16. *A Pain in the Pullman* (6/27/36). Preston Black. Bud Jamison, James C. Morton. The Stooges join a vaudeville troupe traveling by train, and make life hectic for their colleagues. A remake of the Thelma Todd–ZaSu Pitts *Show Business.*

17. *False Alarms* (8/16/36). Del Lord. Stanley Blystone. The boys would rather attend a birthday party than fight fires.

18. *Whoops I'm an Indan* (9/11/36). Del Lord. Bud Jamison. Our con-men heroes have been found out, and in fleeing a lynch mob, take refuge on an Indian reservation.

19. *Slippery Silks* (12/27/36). Preston Black. Vernon Dent, Robert Williams. The Stooges wreck a valuable Chinese cabinet and tangle with its owner.

20. *Grips, Grunts, and Groans* (1/13/37). Preston Black. Harrison Greene, Casey Colombo, Herb Stagman, Chuck Callahan, Blackie Whiteford, Tony Chavez, Elaine Waters, Budd Fine, Sam Lufkin, Everett Sullivan, Bill Irvng, Cy Schindell, Harry Wilson. The Stooges are to guard a wrestler; when he gets away, Curly has to take his place in the ring.

21. *Dizzy Doctors* (3/19/37). Del Lord. June Gittelson, Eva Murray, Ione Leslie, Vernon Dent, Wilfred Lucas, Betty Mac-Mahon, Louise Carver, Bud Jamison, Eric Bunn, Frank Mills, Harley Wood, James C. Morton, A. R. Haysel, Ella McKenzie. The boys go to a local hospital to sell their wonder medicine, "Brighto."

22. *Three Dumb Clucks* (4/17/37). Del Lord. Lynton Brent, Frank Austin. The boys' father wants to leave their mother to marry a gold-digging blonde. Curly plays himself and Father. Remade as *Up in Daisy's Penthouse.*

23. *Back to the Woods* (5/14/37). Preston Black. Bud Jamison, Vernon Dent. In Colonial days, the Stooges are banished into the American wilderness, for a series of encounters with Indians.

24. *Goofs and Saddles* (7/2/37). Del Lord. Ethan Laidlaw, Ted Lorch, Hank Mann, Stanley Blystone, George Gray, Sam Lufkin, Hank Bell. Moe is Wild Bill Hiccup, Curly is Buffalo Billious, and Larry is Just Plain Bill; they disguise as gamblers to bring in a pack of cattle rustlers.

25. *Cash and Carry* (9/3/37). Del Lord. Lester Dorr. The boys try to help a girl and her crippled brother by buying a house with supposed buried treasure in it. Remade by Andy Clyde.

10

A scene from *Dizzy Doctors,* 1937, with Vernon Dent.
The famous short where the Stooges attempt to sell the wonder medicine "Brighto."

26. *Playing the Ponies* (10/15/37). Charles Lamont. William Irving, Jack "Tiny" Lipson. The Stooges buy a broken-down race horse called Thunderbolt.

27. *The Sitter-Downers* (11/26/37). Del Lord. Marcia Healey, Betty Mack, June Gittelson, James C. Morton, Bob McKenzie, Jack Long. When the father of the boys' sweethearts refuses to let them marry, the Stooges go on a sit-down strike.

28. *Termites of 1938* (1/7/38). Del Lord. Dorothy Granger, Bud Jamison, Bess Flowers. The Stooges are mistaken for professional escorts and invited to a society party.

29. *Wee Wee, Monsieur* (2/18/38). Del Lord. Bud Jamison, Vernon Dent. The Stooges accidentally join the French army and encounter problems in the land of Tsimmis.

30. *Tassels in the Air* (4/1/38). Charley Chase. Bess Flowers, Vernon Dent, Bud Jamison. The boys are hired as interior decorators. A partial reworking of Chase's *Luncheon at Twelve.*

31. *Flat Foot Stooges* (5/13/38). Charley Chase. Chester Conklin, Dick Curtis, Lola Jensen. Firemen Moe, Larry, and Curly don't realize that it's their own fire house which is ablaze.

32. *Healthy, Wealthy, and Dumb* (5/20/38). Del Lord. Lucille Lund, James C. Morton, Bud Jamison, Bobby Burns. Curly wins a fortune in a radio contest, and three gold-digging girls move in and try to collect. Remade as *A Missed Fortune*.

33. *Violent Is the Word for Curly* (7/2/38). Charley Chase. Eddie Fetherstone, Gladys Gale, Marjorie Dean, Bud Jamison, John T. Murray, Pat Gleason. The Stooges are mistaken for visiting professors at a girls' school, and teach the girls a nonsense song.

34. *Three Missing Links* (7/29/38). Jules White. Monty Collins, Jane Hamilton, James C. Morton, Naba. The only way the boys can get into the movies is to have Curly don a gorilla suit.

35. *Mutts to You* (10/14/38). Charley Chase. Bess Flowers, Lane Chandler, Vernon Dent, Bud Jamison. The Stooges, professional dog-washers, take home an abandoned baby, which is thought to have been kidnapped.

A scene from *So Long, Mr. Chumps,* 1941.

The Stooges tackle Marjorie Dean, in a scene from *Violent is the Word for Curly*, 1938.

36. *Three Little Sew and Sews* (1/6/39). Del Lord. Harry Semels, Phyllis Barry, James C. Morton, Vernon Dent, Bud Jamison. The boys are mistaken for sailors, Curly for an admiral, as they become involved with an espionage ring. Original title: *Three Goofy Gobs*.

37. *We Want Our Mummy* (2/24/39). Del Lord. Bud Jamison, Jame C. Morton, Dick Curtis, Robert Williams. The Stooges are hired to find an archaeologist who disappeared while seeking the mummy of King Rutentuton.

38. *A-Ducking They Did Go* (4/7/39). Del Lord. Vernon Dent, Bud Jamison. The boys sell memberships in a duck-hunting club on a lake that hasn't seen a duck in years.

39. *Yes, We Have No Bonanza* (5/19/39). Del Lord. Dick Curtis, Lynton Brent, Vernon Dent. The boys abandon their jobs as singing waiters in a saloon to dig for gold.

40. *Saved by the Belle* (6/30/39). Charley Chase. Carmen LaRue, Leroy Mason. While in the tropical region of the globe, the Stooges go into business selling earthquake shock-absorbers.

Curly shows off his medals to Mary Ainslee in *I'll Never Heil Again,* 1941.

41. *Calling All Curs* (8/25/39). Jules White. Lynton Brent. A prize pooch is stolen from the Stooges' dog hospital.

42. *Oily to Bed, Oily to Rise* (10/6/39). Jules White. Dick Curtis, Richard Fiske, Eddie Laughton, Eva McKenzie. The boys discover that crooks have swindled a kindly widow out of a flourishing oil well. Remade as *Oil's Well That Ends Well.*

43. *Three Sappy People* (12/1/39). Jules White. Lorna Gray, Don Beddoe, Bud Jamison, Ann Doran, Richard Fiske. The Stooges, thought to be psychiatrists, are hired by Beddoe to examine his nutty wife.

44. *You Nazty Spy* (1/19/40). Jules White. Dick Curtis, Don Beddoe. A spoof of Hitler and company, with Moe made the dictator of Moronica. Introduction reads, "Any resemblance between the characters in this picture and any persons, living or dead, is a miracle."

45. *Rockin' Through the Rockies* (3/8/40). Jules White. Linda Winters (Dorothy Comingore), Dorothy Appleby, Lorna Gray, Kathryn Sheldon. As medicine show entrepreneurs, the Stooges and their troupe face trouble from Indians and wild bears as they travel west.

14

46. *A-Plumbing We Will Go* (4/19/40). Del Lord. Symona Boniface, Bud Jamison, Bess Flowers, Eddie Laughton. The Stooges try to fix the plumbing in a society mansion, with disastrous results. Remade by El Brendel as *Pick a Peck of Plumbers,* then by the Stooges, using stock footage, as *Vagabond Loafers* and *Scheming Schemers.*

47. *Nutty but Nice* (6/14/40). Jules White. Vernon Dent. The Stooges work to reunite a hospitalized young girl with her father.

48. *How High Is Up?* (7/26/40). Del Lord. Bruce Bennett, Vernon Dent, Edmund Cobb. The boys work as riveters on the 97th story of a building under construction.

49. *From Nurse to Worse* (8/23/40). Jules White. Vernon Dent, Dorothy Appleby. The boys take health insurance on Curly, then try to collect by convincing a doctor that he's crazy.

50. *No Census, No Feeling* (10/4/40). Del Lord. Vernon Dent, Symona Boniface, Max Davidson, Bruce Bennett, Elinor Vandivere. As census takers, the boys go from a bridge party to a football game, all supposedly in the line of duty.

51. *Cuckoo Cavaliers* (11/15/40). Jules White. Dorothy Appleby, Jack O'Shea. The boys buy what they think is a Mexican saloon; it turns out to be a beauty salon.

52. *Boobs in Arms* (12/27/40). Jules White. Richard Fiske, Evelyn Young, Phil Van Zandt. Greeting-card salesmen, the Stooges agree to help out a young lady, unaware that they've already encountered her fuming husband. A partial re-working of Laurel and Hardy's *Fixer-Uppers.*

53. *So Long, Mr. Chumps* (2/7/41). Jules White. Vernon Dent, Bruce Bennett, Robert Williams. The Stooges try to get an "innocent" man out of prison. Footage used in *Beer Barrel Polecats.*

54. *Dutiful but Dumb* (3/21/41). Del Lord. Vernon Dent, Bud Jamison, James C. Morton, Bruce Bennett, Chester Conklin. The Stooges, as photographers Click, Clack, and Cluck, go to the kingdom of Vulgaria.

55. *All the World's a Stooge* (5/16/41). Del Lord. Lelah Tyler, Emory Parnell, Bud Jamison, Symona Boniface, Olaf Hytten, Richard Fiske. A man tries to pass off the Stooges to his wife as "refugee children."

56. *I'll Never Heil Again* (7/11/41). Jules White. Mary Ainslee, John Kascier, Vernon Dent, Bud Jamison. Another Hitler spoof set in Moronica, with a Mata Hari type planting a bomb inside headquarters.

57. *An Ache in Every Stake* (8/22/41). Del Lord. Vernon Dent, Bud Jamison, Gino Corrado, Bess Flowers, Symona Boniface. The Stooges, as icemen, are hired to prepare a fancy birthday dinner.

58. *In the Sweet Pie and Pie* (10/16/41). Jules White. Dorothy Appleby, Mary Ainslee, Ethelreda Leopold, Symona Boniface, Vernon Dent, John Tyrrell, Eddie Laughton. Three society girls marry the Stooges, who are about to be hanged; when they're pardoned, the girls are stuck with them. Includes stock footage with Geneva Mitchell from *Hoi Polloi*. Footage used in *Beer Barrel Polecats*.

59. *Some More of Samoa* (12/4/41). Del Lord. Louise Carver. The boys journey to the island of Rhum Boogie in search of a persimmon tree.

60. *Loco Boy Makes Good* (1/8/42). Jules White. Dorothy Appleby, Vernon Dent, Bud Jamison, Robert Williams. The boys try to save an ailing hotel and its widowed owner, with the help of columnist Waldo Finchell.

61. *Cactus Makes Perfect* (2/26/42). Del Lord. Monty Collins, Vernon Dent, Ernie Adams. The Stooges invent a device that sniffs out gold.

62. *What's the Matador?* (4/23/42). Jules White. Suzanne Kaaren, Harry Burns, Dorothy Appleby, Eddie Laughton. The boys run afoul of a jealous husband just before they are to do a comedy bullfight. Reworked, with stock footage, as *Sappy Bullfighters*.

63. *Matri-Phony* (7/2/42). Harry Edwards. Vernon Dent, Marjorie Deanne. In ancient Erysipelas, the Stooges incur the wrath of their emperor, Octopus Grabus.

64. *Three Smart Saps* (7/30/42). Jules White. Bud Jamison, Barbara Slater, John Tyrrell. The Stooges' fiancées, Stella, Della, and Bella, won't marry them until their father is released from jail.

65. *Even As I.O.U.* (9/18/42). Del Lord. Ruth Skinner, Stanley Blystone, Wheaton Chambers, Vernon Dent, Bud Jamison, Heinie Conklin, Jack Gardner, Billy Bletcher. The boys progress from bookmakers to race-horse owners.

66. *Sock-a-Bye Baby* (11/13/42). Jules White. Bud Jamison, Julie Gibson, Clarence Straight. The boys take in an abandoned baby and then are accused of kidnapping.

67. *They Stooge to Conga* (1/1/43). Del Lord. Vernon Dent. The Stooges, as repairmen, get mixed up with a gang of saboteurs.

68. *Dizzy Detectives* (2/5/43). Jules White. Bud Jamison. The Stooges, as policemen, are assigned to track down a missing gorilla.

69. *Spook Louder* (4/2/43). Del Lord. Stanley Blystone, William Kelly, Symona Boniface. A reporter hears a wild story about the Stooges' adventures while guarding an inventor's eerie house. A remake of Mack Sennett's *The Great Pie Mystery*.

70. *Back from the Front* (5/28/43). Jules White. Vernon Dent, Bud Jamison. During the war, the Stooges (in the Merchant

Moe is about to let Curly have it, in a scene from *Half-Shot Shooters,* 1936.

Marine) encounter two Nazis.

71. *Three Little Twerps* (7/9/43). Harry Edwards. Chester Conklin, Heinie Conklin, Stanley Blystone, Bud Jamison, Duke York. The Stooges barge into a local circus and try to work their way into the proceedings unnoticed.

72. *Higher Than a Kite* (7/30/43). Del Lord. Dick Curtis, Vernon Dent. The Stooges miraculously get inside a bomb which is dropped over Germany; behind German lines, they don disguises and try to get out.

73. *I Can Hardly Wait* (8/13/43). Jules White. Bud Jamison. Curly gets a toothache, and has to visit the dentist.

74. *Dizzy Pilots* (9/24/43). Jules White. Richard Fiske. The Stooges are trying to invent a new plane, but Curly is the one who gets up in the air.

75. *Phony Express* (11/18/43). Del Lord, Shirley Patterson, Chester Conklin, Snub Pollard, Bud Jamison. A Western bandit gang mistakes the Stooges for detectives. Footage used in *Merry Mavericks.*

76. *A Gem of a Jam* (12/30/43). Del Lord. Bud Jamison. The Stooges are janitors in the office of Drs. Harts, Burns, and Belcher, but a trio of crooks think they're the doctors.

77. *Crash Goes the Hash* (2/5/44). Jules White. Vernon Dent, Bud Jamison, Dick Curtis, Symona Boniface. Our three ace reporters act as servants to get the lowdown on a phony nobleman who's going to marry Mrs. Van Bustle.

78. *Busy Buddies* (3/18/44). Del Lord. Vernon Dent, Fred Kelsey. Their short-order restaurant isn't making much money, so the Stooges enter Curly in a cow-milking contest at the State Fair.

79. *The Yoke's on Me* (5/26/44). Jules White. Bob McKenzie. Rejected by the armed services, the boys do their bit in the war by farming.

80. *Idle Roomers* (7/16/44). Del Lord. Christine McIntyre, Duke York, Vernon Dent. The Stooges, as hotel bellboys, are attracted by a pretty blonde, unaware that she's in vaudeville, and there's also a wild gorilla in her room.

81. *Gents Without Cents* (9/22/44). Jules White. Lindsay, Laverne, and Betty. A musical short as the Stooges pair up with a female trio to do a benefit show at a local shipyard.

A scene from *Fright Night,* 1947, the first "short" Shemp made with the Stooges.

18

82. *No Dough, Boys* (11/24/44). Jules White. Vernon Dent, Christine McIntyre. The Stooges, disguised as Japanese, are believed to be the real thing by an underground Nazi group.

83. *Three Pests in a Mess* (1/9/45). Del Lord. Vernon Dent, Vic Travers, Snub Pollard, Christine McIntyre, Brian O'Hara. A gang moves in on the Stooges when it's thought that they've won a sweepstakes.

84. *Booby Dupes* (3/17/45). Del Lord. Rebel Randall, Vernon Dent. With Curly dressed in a navy captain's uniform, the boys go fishing.

85. *Idiots Deluxe* (7/20/45). Jules White. Vernon Dent, Paul Kruger, Gwen Seager, Eddie Laughton. The boys go on a disaster-prone hunting trip; told in flashback, it explains why Moe is on trial for assaulting Larry and Curly.

86. *If a Body Meets a Body* (8/30/45). Jules White. Theodore Lorch, Fred Kelsey. To claim an inheritance, the boys have to spend a night in a creepy old house. Remake of *Laurel-Hardy Murder Case*.

87. *Micro-Phonies* (11/15/45). Edward Bernds. Christine McIntyre, Gino Corrado, Symona Boniface, Fred Kelsey, Sam Flint, Chester Conklin. A society dowager sees the boys pantomiming to one of Christine's records, and hires them to entertain at her party.

88. *Beer Barrel Polecats* (1/10/46). Jules White. Robert Williams, Vernon Dent, Bruce Bennett. The Stooges go to jail for bootlegging, and do their best to escape.

89. *A Bird in the Head* (2/28/46). Edward Bernds. Vernon Dent, Robert Williams, Frank Lackteen. A mad scientist wants to use Curly's "brain" for an experiment.

90. *Uncivil Warbirds* (3/29/46). Jules White. Faye Williams, Eleanor Counts, Marilyn Johnson, Maury Dexter, Ted Lorch, Al Rosen, Blackie Whiteford. The Stooges get caught between both sides in the Civil War.

91. *Three Troubledoers* (4/25/46). Edward Bernds. Christine McIntyre, Dick Curtis, Bud Fine, Hank Bell, Steve Clarke, Ethan Laidlaw, Joe Garcio, Blackie Whiteford. Curly becomes sheriff, Moe and Larry deputies, in a rough western town.

92. *Monkey Businessmen* (6/20/46). Edward Bernds. Kenneth MacDonald, Fred Kelsey, Snub Pollard, Jean Donahue, Cy Schindell, Rocky Woods. The Stooges find themselves in a very shady sanitarium. Remake of a Smith and Dale two-reeler, *Mutiny on the Body*.

93. *Three Loan Wolves* (7/4/46). Jules White. Beverly Warren, Harold Brauer, Wally Rose, Joe Palma. The Stooges, as pawnbrokers ("Here Today, Pawn Tomorrow"), adopt an infant girl.

94. *G.I. Wanna Go Home* (9/5/46). Jules White. Judy Mal-

colm, Ethelreda Leopold, Doris Houck, Symona Boniface. The Stooges, ex-G.I.s, face the postwar housing shortage when they want to get married.

95. *Rhythm and Weep* (10/3/46). Jules White. Jack Norton, Doria Patrice, Ruth Godfrey. Just as they are about to end it all, the Stooges and three girl entertainers are hired for a musical show.

96. *Three Little Pirates* (12/5/46). Edward Bernds. Christine McIntyre. The Stooges, shipwrecked on Dead Man's Island, try to escape from the clutches of The Governor.

97. *Half-Wits Holiday* (1/9/47). Jules White. Vernon Dent, Barbara Slater, Ted Lorch, Emil Sitka, Symona Boniface, Helen Dickson. A professor tries to turn the boys into gentlemen— which results in a pie-throwing melee. A remake of *Hoi Polloi;* stock footage from this film used several times in the future. Curly's last starring film with the Stooges.

98. *Fright Night* (3/6/47). Edward Bernds. Cy Schindell, Dick Wessel, Harold Brauer, Claire Carleton. The Stooges, fight managers, are warned by a gangster that if their man wins, it's curtains for them. Film used almost intact as *Fling in the Ring* several years later. This was Shemp's first short as part of the Stooges.

99. *Out West* (4/24/47). Edward Bernds. Jack Norman (Norman Willis), Jacques (Jock) O'Mahoney, Christine McIntyre, Vernon Dent, Stanley Blystone, George Chesebro, Frank Ellis. The Stooges do their best to foil a dastardly villain, with the help of the Arizona Kid. Final gag repeated years later in the Stooges' feature *The Outlaws Is Coming.*

100. *Hold That Lion* (7/17/47). Jules White. Kenneth Mac-Donald, Emil Sitka, Dudley Dickerson. The boys board a train going after the man who cheated them out of their inheritance. Curly makes a brief gag appearance on the train. Footage used in *Booty and the Beast.*

101. *Brideless Groom* (9/11/47). Edward Bernds. Dee Green, Christine McIntyre, Doris Colleen. Shemp will inherit half a million dollars if he is married within twenty-four hours.

102. *Sing a Song of Six Pants* (10/30/47). Jules White. Dee Green, Harold Brauer, Virginia Hunter. In need of money, the boys try to capture a wanted criminal to get the reward.

103. *All Gummed Up* (12/18/47). Jules White. Christine McIntyre, Emil Sitka. The Stooges invent a youth serum—and it works!

104. *Shivering Sherlocks* (1/8/48). Del Lord. The Stooges accompany a girl to the spooky old mansion she's inherited.

105. *Pardon My Clutch* (2/26/48). Edward Bernds. Matt McHugh, Emil Sitka. The boys want to go on vacation for the benefit of Shemp's frazzled nerves, but all their plans go amuck.

106. *Squareheads of the Round Table* (3/4/48). Edward Bernds. Phil Van Zandt, Vernon Dent, Jacques O'Mahoney, Christine McIntyre, Harold Brauer, Joe Garcia. The boys, troubadors in King Arthur's Court, help their friend the blacksmith foil the evil Black Prince. Remade, with stock footage, as *Knutzy Knights*.

107. *Fiddlers Three* (5/6/48). Jules White. Vernon Dent, Phil Van Zandt, Virginia Hunter. As Old King Cole's fiddlers, the Stooges come to the aid of their kingdom when the Princess is kidnapped.

108. *Heavenly Daze* (9/2/48). Jules White. Vernon Dent, Sam McDaniel. Shemp dies, but he can't enter Heaven until he goes back to earth and reforms Moe and Larry. Remade, using stock footage, as *Bedlam in Paradise*.

109. *Hot Scots* (7/8/48). Edward Bernds. Herbert Evans, Christine McIntyre, Ted Lorch, Charles Knight. Passing themselves off as detectives, the Stooges guard a "haunted" castle in Scotland. Remade, with stock footage, as *Scotched in Scotland*.

110. *I'm a Monkey's Uncle* (10/7/48). Jules White. Dee Green, Virginia Hunter. In caveman days, the Stooges pursue three lovelies named Aggie, Maggie, and Baggie. Remade with stock footage as *Stone Age Romeos*.

111. *Mummy's Dummies* (11/4/48). Edward Bernds. Dee Green, Phil Van Zandt, Ralph Dunn, Vernon Dent. The Stooges are used-chariot dealers in ancient Egypt.

112. *Crime on Their Hands* (12/9/48). Edward Bernds. Kenneth MacDonald, Christine McIntyre, Charles C. Wilson, Lester Allen. In trying to track down a stolen diamond, Shemp accidentally swallows it.

113. *The Ghost Talks* (2/3/49). Jules White. The Stooges are moving men assigned to an ancient castle where they meet the ghost of Peeping Tom. Footage used in *Creeps*.

114. *Who Done It?* (3/3/49). Edward Bernds. Christine McIntyre, Kenneth MacDonald, Symona Boniface, Emil Sitka, Dudley Dickerson, Herbert Evans. The Stooges, as private detectives, are supposed to protect a millionaire from the clutches of a gang.

115. *Hocus Pocus* (5/5/49). Jules White. Mary Ainslee, Vernon Dent, Jimmy Lloyd. The boys become flagpole-walkers under the influence of Svengarlic, the Magician.

116. *Fuelin' Around* (7/7/49). Edward Bernds. Jacques O'Mahoney, Christine McIntyre, Emil Sitka, Vernon Dent, Phil Van Zandt. Shemp, mistaken for a scientist, is abducted to a foreign kingdom along with Moe and Larry:

117. *Malice in the Palace* (9/1/49). Jules White. George Lewis, Frank Lackteen, Vernon Dent. The boys set out to recover a famous diamond that rests somewhere in Egypt.

A scene from *He Cooked His Goose,* 1952, with Angela Stevens.

118. *Vagabond Loafers* (10/6/49). Edward Bernds. Christine McIntyre, Kenneth MacDonald, Symona Boniface, Emil Sitka, Dudley Dickerson, Herbert Evans. While fixing the plumbing in a society mansion, the Stooges get involved with some clever thieves. A reworking of *A-Plumbing We Will Go,* with some stock footage from *Half-Wits Holiday.* Used almost intact several years later as *Scheming Schemers.*

119. *Dunked in the Deep* (11/3/49). Jules White. Gene Stutenroth (Roth). The Stooges get involved in a spy hunt involving some microfilm.

120. *Punchy Cowpunchers* (1/5/50). Edward Bernds. Jacques O'Mahoney, Christine McIntyre, Dick Wessel, Kenneth MacDonald, Vernon Dent, Emil Sitka. The Stooges work incognito for the United States Cavalry. Note: This and several subsequent shorts have been incorrectly credited to Hugh McCollum, who produced them.

121. *Hugs and Mugs* (2/2/50). Jules White. Christine McIntyre, Nanette Bordeaux, Kathleen O'Malley, Emil Sitka. The Stooges go on a frantic search for some missing pearls.

122. *Dopey Dicks* (3/2/50). Edward Bernds. Christine McIntyre, Stanley Price, Phil Van Zandt. The Stooges encounter a scientist on the lookout for a brain he can use for his experimental robot.

123. *Love at First Bite* (5/4/50). Jules White. Christine McIntyre, Yvette Reynard, Marie Montiel. The Stooges are awaiting the arrival of the sweethearts they met during the war in France.

124. *Self-Made Maids* (7/6/50). Hugh McCollum. Each Stooge plays four parts in this film, depicting blossoming romance between three artists and their models.

125. *Three Hams on Rye* (9/7/50). Jules White. Nanette Boardman, Emil Sitka, Christine McIntyre. The Stooges, prop-men in a theatre, finally get a chance to go on stage.

126. *Studio Stoops* (10/5/50). Edward Bernds. Kenneth MacDonald, Stanley Price, Vernon Dent. Publicists for the B.O. Movie Studio, the Stooges try to foil the kidnapping of one of their stars.

127. *Slap Happy Sleuths* (11/9/50). Hugh McCollum. Stanley Blystone, Emil Sitka, Gene Roth. The Stooges investigate the Great Onion Oil Company robbery.

128. *A Snitch in Time* (12/7/50). Edward Bernds. Jean Willes. Furniture dealers, the Stooges get tangled up with jewel thieves.

129. *Three Arabian Nuts* (1/4/51). Edward Bernds. Vernon Dent, Phil Van Zandt, Dick Curtis, Wesley Bly. The Stooges acquire a lamp with an obliging genie inside.

130. *Baby Sitters Jitters* (2/1/51). Jules White. Lynn Davis, David Windsor, Margie Liszt, Myron Healey. A baby is snatched from under the Stooges' noses as they're supposed to be baby-sitting.

131. *Don't Throw That Knife* (5/3/51). Jules White. Dick Curtis, Jean Willes. The Stooges are census takers who just seem to get tangled up more than they should with their interviewees.

132. *Scrambled Brains* (7/7/51). Jules White. Babe London, Emil Sitka, Vernon Dent. Shemp is suffering from hallucinations.

133. *Merry Mavericks* (9/6/51). Edward Bernds. Dan Harvey, Mary Martin, Paul Campbell. The Stooges are medicine-show con men mistaken for fearless lawmen by a gang of toughs. Uses footage from *Phony Express*.

134. *The Tooth Will Out* (10/4/51). Edward Bernds. Margie Liszt, Vernon Dent. The Stooges are none-too-efficient dentists. Original title: *A Yank at the Dentist.*

135. *Hula La La* (11/1/51). Hugh McCollum. Jean Willes, Joy Windsor, Kenneth MacDonald, Emil Sitka. The boys are dancing teachers sent to a South Sea island on assignment.

136. *The Pest Man Wins* (12/6/51). Jules White. Margie Liszt, Nanette Bordeaux, Emil Sitka, Vernon Dent, Helen Dickson, Symona Boniface. The Stooges as exterminators who bring their own insects with them. A remake of *Ants in the Pantry,* with stock footage from *Half-Wits' Holiday.*

137. *A Missed Fortune* (1/3/52). Jules White. Nanette

Bordeaux, Vivian Mason, Vernon Dent. Three gold-digging girls pounce on Shemp when they learn he's won a radio contest. Remake of *Healthy, Wealthy, and Dumb.*

138. *Listen, Judge* (3/6/52). Edward Bernds. Emil Sitka, Vernon Dent, Kitty McHugh. The Stooges are short-order cooks in trouble with the law.

139. *Corny Casanovas* (5/1/52). Jules White. Connie Cezan. Moe, Larry, and Shemp are all in love with the same girl, but they don't know it. Remade, with stock footage, as *Rusty Romeos.*

140. *He Cooked His Goose* (7/3/52). Jules White. Mary Ainslee, Angela Stevens. Larry is two-timing Moe's wife and Shemp's fiancée at the same time. Remade, with stock footage, as *Triple Crossed.*

141. *Gents in a Jam* (7/4/52). Edward Bernds. David Bond, Mary Ainslee, Vernon Dent, Emil Sitka, Kitty McHugh, Mickey Simpson, Dany Sue Nolan. The Stooges try to collect a legacy.

142. *Three Dark Horses* (10/16/52). Jules White. Kenneth MacDonald, Ben Welden. The Stooges get involved with crooked politics.

143. *Cuckoo on a Choo Choo* (12/4/52). Jules White. Patricia Wright, Victoria Horne. The Stooges are stuck on an abandoned train car.

144. *Up in Daisy's Penthouse* (2/5/53). Jules White. Connie Cezan, John Merton, Jack Kenny. The boys' pa wants to marry a young girl—who turns out to be a gun moll. Shemp plays himself and Pa. A remake of *Three Dumb Clucks.*

145. *Booty and the Beast* (3/5/53). Jules White. Kenneth MacDonald, Vernon Dent. The boys unintentionally help a man commit a robbery.

146. *Loose Loot* (4/2/53). Jules White. Kenneth MacDonald, Tom Kennedy, Emil Sitka. Their lawyer, from Cess, Poole, and Drayne, tells the boys they will have to subpeona MacDonald to get their inheritance from him.

147. *Tricky Dicks* (5/7/53). Jules White. Benny Rubin, Connie Cezan, Ferris Taylor, Phil Arnold, Murray Alper. The Stooges go to jail to find their man.

148. *Spooks* (6/15/53). Jules White. Phil Van Zandt, Tom Kennedy, Norma Randall. Posing as pie salesmen, the detective Stooges invade a mad scientist's spooky hideout. Filmed in 3-D.

149. *Pardon My Backfire* (8/15/53). Jules White. Benny Rubin, Frank Sully, Phil Arnold, Fred Kelsey. The Stooges, proprietors of a garage, encounter three crooks on the lam. Filmed in 3-D.

150. *Rip Sew and Stitch* (9/3/53). Jules White. Vernon Dent, Phil Arnold. The boys are tailors who find one of their mannequins has come to life—or so it seems, with a criminal on the loose.

151. *Bubble Trouble* (10/8/53). Jules White. Emil Sitka, Christine McIntyre. A youth serum that works for an old woman backfires on her husband. Overlapping from *All Gummed Up*, using some footage.

152. *Goof on the Roof* (12/3/53). Jules White. The Stooges try to install a television aerial.

153. *Income Tax Sappy* (2/4/54). Jules White. Benny Rubin, Margie Liszt, Nanette Bordeaux. The boys do so well cheating on their income tax that they decide to go into business doing it.

154. *Musty Musketeers* (5/13/54). Jules White. Vernon Dent, Phil Van Zandt. The boys help rescue an abducted princess.

155. *Pal and Gals* (6/3/54). Jules White. Christine McIntyre, George Chesebro. Norman Willis, Heinie Conklin, Vernon Dent. The Stooges go west, and come to the aid of defenseless Little Nell.

156. *Knutzy Knights* (9/2/54). Jules White. Jacques O'Mahoney, Christine McIntyre, Phil Van Zandt. A remake, with stock footage, of *Squareheads of the Round Table*.

157. *Shot in the Frontier* (10/7/54). Jules White. Rivalry over women brings the Stooges to a shoot-out in the old West.

A very young Shemp Howard in the middle, as he appeared in an independent film without the Stooges. Dick Wessel is on the right.

158. *Scotched in Scotland* (11/4/54). Jules White. Phil Van Zandt, Christine McIntyre, Charles Knight. The Stooges are assigned to detective work in a haunted castle. Remake, with stock footage, of *Hot Scots.*

159. *Fling in the Ring* (1/6/55). Jules White. Richard Wessel, Claire Carleton, Frank Sully. The Stooges, as fight managers, are warned against success by the head man in the racket. Remake with much footage from *Fright Night.*

160. *Of Cash and Hash* (2/3/55). Jules White. Kenneth Mac-Donald, Christine McIntyre, Frank Lackteen. Restaurant owners Moe, Larry, and Shemp get involved with gangsters.

161. *Gypped in the Penthouse* (3/10/55). Jules White. Jean Willes, Emil Sitka. The boys fall for a gold digger.

162. *Bedlam in Paradise* (4/14/55). Jules White. Phil Van Zandt, Sylvia Lewis, Vernon Dent, Symona Boniface. Shemp dies, goes to Heaven, but can't be admitted until he reforms Moe and Larry. Virtually the same film, with most of the footage, as *Heavenly Daze.*

163. *Stone Age Romeos* (6/2/55). Jules White. Emil Sitka, Dee Green, Nancy Saunders, Virginia Hunter. A new framework for footage from *I'm a Monkey's Uncle.*

164. *Wham Bam Slam* (9/1/55). Jules White. Matt McHugh, Alyn Loar, Dora Revier, Wanda Perry. The boys and their family go on a camping trip. Overlapping *Pardon My Clutch,* using some of its footage.

165. *Hot Ice* (10/6/55). Jules White. Kenneth MacDonald, Christine McIntyre. The Stooges are Scotland Yard detectives after the Punjab diamond.

166. *Blunder Boys* (11/3/55). Jules White. Benny Rubin, Angela Stevens, Kenneth MacDonald. The Stooges, as police sergeants Holiday, Two-a-Day, and Labor Day, track down a gunman disguised as a woman.

167. *Husbands Beware* (1/5/56). Jules White. Emil Sitka, Christine McIntyre. Moe and Larry, both henpecked, don't see why Shemp shouldn't be in the same boat.

168. *Creeps* (2/2/56). Jules White. The Stooges play their own sons. They relate to the kids their adventures in a haunted castle. Includes stock footage from *The Ghost Talks.*

169. *Flagpole Jitters* (4/5/56). Jules White. Beverly Thomas, Barbara Bartay, Mary Ainslee, Bonnie Menjum, Don Harvey, David Bond, Frank Sully, Dick Alexander. Remake, with stock footage, of *Hocus Pocus.*

170. *For Crimin' Out Loud* (5/3/56). Jules White. Barbara Bartay, Emil Sitka, Christine McIntyre, Duke York, Charles Knight. The boys try to rescue a kidnapped politician.

171. *Rumpus in the Harem* (6/21/56). Jules White. Harriette Tarler, Diana Darrin, Helen Jay, Ruth Godfrey White, Suzanne

Ridgeway. The Stooges dare to protect three lovelies from servitude under the Sultan.

172. *Hot Stuff* (9/6/56). Jules White. Emil Sitka, Christine McIntyre, Connie Cezan, Evelyn Lovequist, Andri Pola, Vernon Dent, Harold Brauer. The Stooges try to protect a professor (who has a top-secret rocket fuel formula) and his daughter.

173. *Scheming Schemers* (10/4/56). Jules White. Christine McIntyre, Kenneth MacDonald, Symona Boniface, Emil Sitka, Dudley Dickerson, H. Coons. Virtually the same film as *Vagabond Loafers,* which itself was a remake of *A-Plumbing We Will Go,* with stock footage from *Half-Wits Holiday.*

174. *Commotion on the Ocean* (11/8/56). Jules White. Gene Roth, Harriette Tarler. The Stooges go to sea to track down a spy ring. Shemp's last film with the Stooges.

175. *Hoofs and Goofs* (1/31/57). Jules White. Benny Rubin, Harriette Tarler. The Stooges' sister is reincarnated as a horse! This was Joe Besser's first short with the Stooges.

A scene from *Hoofs and Goofs,* 1957, Joe Besser's first short with the Stooges. The horse is supposedly the Stooges' sister reincarnated.

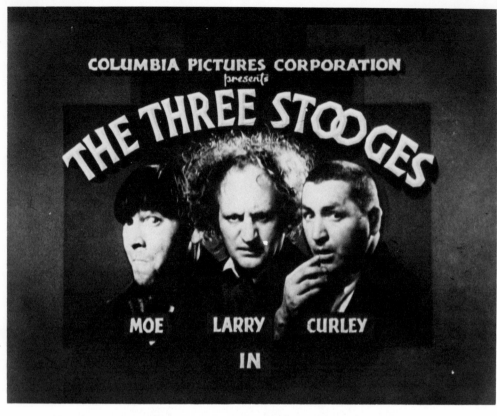

COLUMBIA PICTURES CORPORATION
presents

THE THREE STOOGES

MOE   LARRY   CURLEY

IN

The familiar Columbia "logo" used to introduce most of the early Three Stooges' shorts.

176. *Muscle Up a Little Closer* (2/28/57). Jules White. Maxine Gates, Ruth Godfrey White, Matt Murphy, Harriette Tarler. The Stooges play identical triplets, which creates havoc for everyone.

177. *A Merry Mix-Up* (3/28/57). Jules White. Nanette Bordeaux, Jeanne Carmen, Ruth Godfrey White, Suzanne Ridgeway, Harriette Tarler, Diana Darrin. The Stooges play identical triplets.

178. *Space Ship Sappy* (4/18/57). Jules White. Benny Rubin, Emil Sitka, Lorraine Crawford, Harriette Tarler, Marilyn Hanold, Doreen Woodbury. The boys travel to a strange planet inhabited by beautiful Amazons.

179. *Guns A-Poppin* (6/13/57). Jules White. Frank Sully, Joe Palma, Vernon Dent. Vacationing in a cabin in the woods, the Stooges get involved with a bandit, a sheriff, and a grizzly bear.

180. *Horsing Around* (9/12/57). Jules White. Emil Sitka, Tony the Wonder Horse, Harriette Tarler. A sequel to *Hoofs and Goofs* with their sister-horse trying to save her husband from the glue factory.

181. *Rusty Romeos* (10/17/57). Jules White. Connie Cezan. The Stooges are all in love with the same girl, only they don't know it. A remake of *Corny Casanovas,* with stock footage.

182. *Outer Space Jitters* (12/5/57). Jules White. Emil Sitka, Gene Roth, Phil Van Zandt, Joe Palma, Dan Blocker, Harriette Tarler, Diana Darrin, Arline Hunter. The boys fly to the planet Zunev and meet some girls with electricity in their veins.

183. *Quiz Whiz* (2/13/58). Jules White. Greta Thyssen, Gene Roth, Milton Frome, Bill Brauer, Emil Sitka. Joe wins a big TV jackpot, then loses it to a gang of swindlers.

184. *Fifi Blows Her Top* (4/10/58). Jules White. Vanda Dupre, Phil Van Zandt, Harriette Tarler, Joe Palma. Joe discovers that his old heart throb, Fifi, is now married and living across the hall.

185. *Pies and Guys* (6/12/58). Jules White. Greta Thyssen, Gene Roth, Milton Frome, Helen Dickson, John Kascier, Harriette Tarler, Symona Boniface. A remake of *Half-Wits' Holiday,* using stock footage.

186. *Sweet and Hot* (9/4/58). Jules White. Muriel Landers. A musical short featuring Muriel as Joe's sister and Moe as a psychiatrist who tries to help her.

187. *Flying Saucer Daffy* (10/9/58). Jules White. Harriette Tarler, Emil Sitka, Gail Bonney, Bek Nelson, Diana Darrin. Joe wins a contest taking a photo of a phony flying saucer—and then encounters a real one.

188. *Oil's Well That Ends Well* (12/4/58). Jules White. A remake, with stock footage, of *Oily to Bed, Oily to Rise.*

189. *Triple Crossed* (2/2/59). Jules White. Angela Stevens, Mary Ainsley, Diana Darrin. Larry tries to cross up Moe and Joe with their girl friends. A remake, with stock footage, of *He Cooked His Goose.*

190. *Sappy Bullfighters* (6/4/59). Jules White. Greta Thyssen, George Lewis. The boys do their comedy bullfight act in Mexico, and run afoul of a beautiful blonde's husband. A remake, with stock footage, of *What's the Matador.*

And Now For Something Completely STOOGIST...

Charles Aitel

STOOGE MANTRA

O holy trinity of trivial profundity
Three-formed divinity of sacramental slapstick
Holy holy holy Curly Joe Larry and Moe
Three befuddled fates three sacred basket cases
A mystic Indian tryptych of the goofy gods of life
Blessed be their fall

Holy Curly Joe with the body of Brahma
Fat and majestic sleek and satisfied
Shining like the noontime light
Glowing empty noggin bald and sunbright
Egg of creation at the earths' birth
Sacred addlepated bald creator
Fumbler bumbler knocking the row of dominoes
Bringer of catastrophe and primal stooge
Holy Brahma Curly Joe
Set the world in motion and fell flat on his ass

Cloud-haired Larry takes Curly's cake
Slips and shoves it in the destroyer's face
Scatterbrained Larry innocent Vishnu
Incompetent sustainer slipping down the drain
Well-meaning moron nervous and fussy
Butt of jokes taffy-headed buffoon
Frizzy hair sparks like a thousand short circuits
Crazy Larry Vishnu the stupid
Blessed be the holy halfbaked clown

Now comes the black-locked power of darkness
Out of the void he trips and falls
Moe the destroyer Moe the avenger
Beatle-wigged Siva balanced on a banana
Puts the world to rest with a conk on the head
Saluting the world with a two-fingered mudra

A poke in the eyes and a slap to the jaw
Leveler of laws destroyer of sanity
Gives the world a shake
Says wake up and go to sleep

Holy holy holy Curly Joe Larry and Moe
Bumbling plumbers in the basement of the soul
Fools and stooges cosmic fall guys
Schlemiels with the real world as their soup
Holy gods with sacred faces
Grimaces and grins with meaningless meanings
Thrice-great geeks in a sacred crazyhouse
Holy Moe Holy Larry Holy Holy Curly Joe

Jean Alford

WORLD SERIES

The next one goes to
the plate while the one
on third scratches his head
trying to figure out
where fourth base is.

There are now three
billion stooges batting
flies and walking to first.

Blythe Ayne

SEISMOGRAPH: MODIFIED MERCALLI SCALE
(found poem—San Francisco science museum)

1. Not felt by people except under especially favorable conditions.

2. Felt indoors by a few people, especially on the upper floors of multi-storied buildings.

3. Felt indoors by several people, usually as a rapid vibration that may not be recognized as an earthquake at first.

4. Felt indoors by many, outdoors by a few. It may waken light sleepers, but isn't apt to frighten anyone. Dishes rattle, and small cracks often appear in plaster walls.

5. Felt indoors by nearly everyone, outdoors by most. It awakens many and frightens a few people. Some persons run outside, fragile items are broken and pendulum clocks run fast or slow.

6. Felt by everyone, inside and out. It awakens all sleepers and creates general excitement. Bells ring, some buildings are damaged, and many are frightened.

7. Everyone is frightened and alarm is general. Most people try to get out of buildings. Trees move crazily and poorly constructed buildings are severely damaged.

8. There is general alarm, approaching panic. Sand and mud erupt in small amounts, branches break off trees, chimneys collapse, most construction is damaged and natural water flow in springs and wells is noticeably altered.

9. Panic is general and the ground shifts and cracks conspicuously. Many masonry buildings collapse, wooden ones are distorted.

10. There are landslides, destroyed foundations, distorted railroad rails and badly damaged highways. Panic is general.

11. Panic is general. Underground pipes and cables are severed or crushed. Oceanic waves of destructive magnitude may develop.

12. Panic is general. Destruction is total.

guy r. beining

ARTISM

as to why
we gathered
here   dot
i don   comma   t
remember
well let   comma   s
say it   comma   s
time to leave   dot

John Bennett

Dear Friends & Relatives
             & all potential
visitors:
         just dust off your shoes
       & step right up
            click your heels
       & set your teeth
            keep a hand on your
                   wallets
       & watch the bumps
              hang on to the
              handrail for dear life
       don't go glancing around
                   what the fuck
         do you think this is,
                    an Easter Parade?

Steven Ford Brown

GEORGE MEETS RICHARD NIXON

George reached California
& on the beach in San Clemente
met Richard Nixon who
limped up to him
& told him that he wasn't a liar
that he wasn't really
that he told the truth too
only his cherry tree
was a California redwood
that stretched 200 feet
into the air & when he
tried to cut it down
it fell on him

GEORGE & THE AMERICAN DOLLAR

George looked out over
the Potomac   wind at
the nape of his neck like
a second pony tail
he threw a silver dollar
across the river
it devalued three times
in its journey over
to the other side
& hit a sailor
in the eye

GEORGE READS *ON THE ROAD*

like Kerouac & Cassidy
George & John Adams
pile into a '56 Chevy
& haulass across the country
drinking cherry wine
& smoking marijuana

George berates the radio
pounding it with an 18th century hand
demanding "real music"
the radio reaches out into a dark pocket
somewhere in the air & pulls out
a minuet covered with a slow dust

THE MAGICIAN

on a little road
near Golgotha
Jesus is performing His magic show
He pulls rabbits & pure white doves
from His tophat
& performs sleight of hand tricks
with gold coins
that knocks the crowds out

while Jesus
makes a bowl of goldfish
disappear
carpenters
are building
three
crosses

Terry W. Brown

TRUTH

Truth
is harder to find,
than it was
when I was small,
and always told
on myself.

Fool
you say
as you point
your finger,
if indeed
that is a finger.

Terry W. Brown

ACROPHOBIA

My wife's acrophobia
is really causing problems,
you see she has
this terrible fear
of being landed on
by a falling acrobat.

So you say, big deal,
stay away from the circus.

Well, that's not so easy
when you're the only clowns.

Kermit Coad

THE TRUTH IS

They say Handel
shut himself up
in a room
for days without food
or water to
write
the Messiah.
It will take
me ex
actly 30 seconds
to finish this
poem.
If you look closely
enough,
you can
probably
even see
where I
dropped
my bacon
sandwich.

Gene Casaretto

IN ANTICIPATION OF THE
THREE STOOGES' FILM FESTIVAL

and
i just know that
some
loosed Laughter
has been floating
galactically free
through space
heading straight for you
since before you ever existed
waiting for that perfect moment
next sunday
when it will
find your mouth, tongue,
and head
unguarded
and deliciously
come to stay.

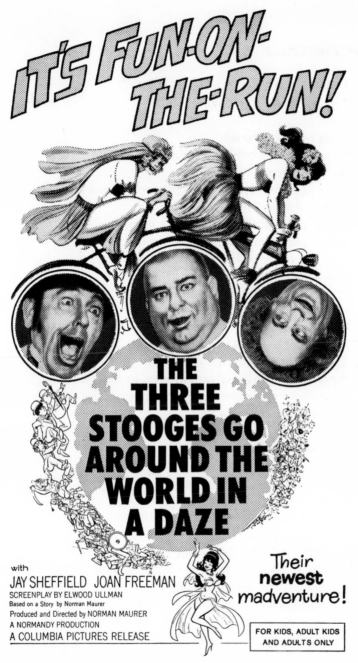

An ad from a Columbia Pressbook promoting one of the Stooges'
feature films made in 1963 which starred Joe DeRita as Curly-Joe.

Jane Conant-Bissell

I THOT THAT YOU WOULD BE
THERE BUT YOU WERE NOT

I was never prepared
taking with me only Ethiopian hair tonic
and one galosh
never never in my life was I properly prepared
white-robed relief maps briefed me
in the lobby of Outer Mongolia Airlines
before taking my soupbone from me
but they never really told me the purpose
or what to expect next
when I finally found the underground bath
I thought you would be there
but you were not
my nickels turned into dentures
and I could not pay the price
the second time a seal pup dressed as Mary Lincoln
suggested that we sneak in through the boys' bathroom
but I had lost my towel
never no not one time that I can think of
was I adequately prepared
the wind turned against me
or the rain dropped lollipops
when I had brought my soap
and now how can I anticipate tomorrow
how can I say "Sure Jack I'll go with you"
when the last time I did that
you took me to a wrestling match between female baboons
and they chose me to referee
but nobody ever explained the rules?

Art Cuelho

MONEY TALKS

Money talks like
death without a hardon;
I got more money
than pickles have bras.

47

Geoffrey Cook

Ode
To the Three Stooges

Ode
To the Three Stooges

DD-4182-5

A crazy scene from *Up in Daisy's Penthouse,* 1953, with John Merton, Connie Cezan and Jack Kenny.

Dorell DiRicco

NEXT TIME THE WOODWORK
GETS PAINTED FINGERPRINT GREY

i woke up cold
and wondered how i got in
the refrigerator
decided to get out
before it started cleaning itself

that's it
today was going to be different
i grabbed the feather duster
and whipped it over the breakfast dishes
before he had a chance to
drink up all my hours
smoothing them out
with his non-committant committance
he stretched out his hand
trying to get a hold on my sanity
but i jumped on a pinwheel
spun round and round
throwing pot holders at him
saying
not now
i'm right in the middle of a rothschilds

John Ditsky

THE CATS OF HAMILTON

The cats of Hamilton that left
the public gaze a while
returned eventually, quite
changed, as Chinese food.

(These things will happen. If
you have a yen for yowler
kow or meow chow *mein,*
you may not even mind . . .)

Considering chicken's cost,
it's hardly simple cheapness
causing this chef's surprise.
Let's look beneath the rice:

Culture of carved ivory,
theirs—these cooks'—is a way
of seeing that takes the bone
for precious, meat as dross.

To free the frame within!
Reducing the alley ruffian
to a box picked clean
of inessential matter—

what recipes so fine? Get
to the basic forms of things:
articulated hatred in a skull
and skeleton, acceptance, Tao.

Joe M. Fericano

COMMENT

In the distance of
faraway plans
lie several obstacles
in which
one encounters such periods
as
the lack of time achieved
in getting there.

To get there
one must have efficient
time to encounter
the obstacles
which lie faraway
in the distance of the plan.

In conclusion
I myself
don't make very many plans.

Kevin FitzPatrick

Dear_____,

Dear _____,

I have personally selected you and a small party of others
from a lenthy directory of compassionate persons to re-
ceive the following invitation:

>You are invited out tonight,
>I don't care what the weather is.
>That's right, you!
>Busses have been rented,
>CBS will be there,
>Phalen field, 9 o'clock,
>And with the others all at once
>In your best clothes
>(NO JEANS OR SLACKS)
>In your loudest voice
>You will admit,
>"I apologize, Kevin,
>>for making you feel rotten."

I am looking forward to seeing you tonight, _____,
Afterwards, I might add, before boarding the busses, freetime
will be available for apologies to each other.

>Be loving,

>Kevin

The Stooges entertain the jury in a scene from *Disorder in the Court,* 1936.

Paul F. Fericano

THE THREE STOOGES DO A TV SERIES

the three stooges finally get
their own tv series called:
RICH STOOGE, POOR STOOGE
but
the studio makes a mistake and
bills them as
groucho
harpo and
chico

when the stooges complain
the studio apologizes and
bills them as
laurel & hardy plus
milton berle

when the stooges threaten to
sue
the studio gives in and
bill them as
abbott & costello plus
don rickles

the stooges take the matter to court where the
judge (who happens to be
related to both milton berle *and*
don rickles) decides they
should be billed as
kukla
fran and
ollie
and then cancels their show

(an appeal filed by the
late jack benny
is denied)

57

Paul F. Fericano

THE THREE STOOGES ON THE L.A. FREEWAY

the three stooges are
traveling down the
los angeles freeway in the
back seat of a '39 ford
smoking cigars
and no one is driving

dirty harry (who has been
demoted to a motorcycle cop)
pulls them over
draws his .44 magnum
squints his eyes and asks:
"just what the hell do you
three punks think you're doing?"

"55 in the slow lane" moe explains
"60 in the fast lane" larry disagrees
"5 to 10 in san quentin" curly says

dirty harry just can't
take anymore shit and he
finally freaks out
he yanks off his
badge
throws it away
runs back to his
motorcycle
tells it to freeze
backs it up against the
guardrail and then
shoots it dead as he runs
screaming hysterically
across the freeway
getting hit by a
rented car from hertz driven by
o.j. simpson who is trying to
pick up an extra 500 yards
before the game

A scene from *Oily to Bed, Oily to Rise,* 1939.

Al Fogel

ROBOT

circuitry set.
plug in.
press button.
output:
jesus saves.
stop.
wait for response.
negative response.
continue output:
jesus is the only way.
stop.
give time to react.
negative reaction.
continue output:
you are going to hell.
stop.
wait for response.
negative response.
stop.
move to next sinner.
press button.
output:
jesus saves.
stop.
wait for response.
positive response.
continue output:
yes brother hallelujah amen.
stop.
place both arms around brother.
hug brother tightly.
stop.

report to headquarters
let disciple record numerical input.
hug disciple.
stop.
go to sleepquarters.
lay down.
recite prayer.
unplug.

Don Foster

SHEMP'S LAMENT

I find now
that I'm less at ease
than I was five years ago
and five years ago
I was in a sanitarium
in Colorado
left there overnight
by friends
who even crazier than me
(dare I say it, one of them
my brother)
by noon had forgotten where
they had deposited me
(or had they just forgotten me
entirely)

luckily I broke out and kept
on the run,
whether away from
or towards my friends
I can't remember
maybe my brother
was right after all,
taking dishwashing jobs
here and there
given to unpredictable spells
of meeb meeb meeb meeb meeb

and then there was the matter
of my snap-on face
and the night the police
tried to pull it off
it's snap-on but permanent
I told them always informative

my brother came out of a chili
house and was so surprised
to see me he advised the cops
to spread out before affectionately
slapping my cheek with his open hand

listen you mug I told him
but he wasn't listening
what about Boulder Colorado
Boulder Colorado he screamed
I'd stuck a nerve
slowly I turned, step by step
he informed me
it was an old act
and I would end up being mauled

A scene from *Commotion on the Ocean*, 1956. This was Shemp's last film with the Stooges.

so I snapped on my snap-on face
hard against my skull
and he jumped back like a child
and I made my escape thru a sewer
never really chased; my brother's
attention span was too brief
until I came here, overlooking
swimming pools and reefs
and meeb meeb meeb meeb meeb
my spells got worse
and children took me for
a lost uncle, not eccentric
they said, not mad, I just
hadn't found my way
and not until the foul
odors seeped from under my snap-
on face did they come to realize
that a man rules his destiny
by his pretentions and that a lost
uncle, mad, eccentric, or otherwise
is still a man who can weep
for small things and who can die
for even smaller things, bullets or emotions

Don Foster

MOE'S BLUES

Moe buys a saxophone.
Listen to this he says.
He sounds like Charlie Parker.
Nyuk nyuk nyuk says Curly.
Moe hits him with his sax.
Now it looks like Dizzy's
Crazy Flugelhorn.
Out of every little pretender
Who fails in his illusion
There crawls another pretender
On a somewhat lower scale.

Hugh Fox

THANGS AMERICAN

26.

AM TRAK
Kansas City to Chicago
through Missouri jungles, over Mississippi mud,
I keep thinking of this fellow-RR-man (3 months
from retirement) buddy of my retired RR-man father-in-
law who came over to the
house last night and we had
pecan and peach pie and ice cream
and coffee,
and because I'd written this book about Indians
he more or less
"interviewed"
me on The Big Ones—
the *where* of the origin of man,
the *how-long* of man in America,
the *how-possible* of prehistoric
contact between the Americas, Asia,
the Mediterranean,
and his wife, who teaches
retarded children, talked about
teaching and retardation,
testing and the Great American Push
toward high stands ("In spite of the
NAACP," said my father-in-law).
She came off almost TELL IT LIKE IT IS,
but him, in his earnest plastic
white shoes, jolly good fellow polyester no-
belt slacks and carefully
butterfly-collared
sports-shirt . . . .
after he left my
mother-in-law said "He's

really a very good-looking guy, but . . ."
And my father-in-law
took over "Down at work he
takes out his teeth, wears this
jacket with one sleeve all torn, wears
the same old overalls he's had for years . . . and don't
know nothin', brother, he's *dumb,* which is really
playing it smart."

Kevin Goldstein-Jackson

WORDS

Abreption, absterge, alabaster,
Allochroic, amaranthine, bacchanal,
Collimate, diaphanous, evanesce,
Flaccid, flummery, glabrous,
Hebetude, hyaline, ipecacuanha,
Jocose, kindliness, lazzarone,
Leonine, maffick, mansuetude,
Minatory, nuncupate, nympholepsy,
Obfuscate, odalisque, osculate,
Pantology, pasquinade, pizzicato,
Plethora, quintessence, refulgent,
Rhadamanthine, scrimshank, sforzando,
Tellurian, thaumaturge, undine,
Uxorious, vermilion, vulpine,
Wormwood, xyloid, yielding, zoom —
(My A to Z kaleidoscope of words.)

Don A. Hoyt

BAHAMA VACATION

I knew an old man
who left his dog and grand-kids
for a soaring, semi-conscious cruise
to the Bahamas on a jet,
that roared him off one midnight
from New Orleans International
after a two hour lay-over,
though he sat through most of it
or browsed the air port shops,
seeking souveniers to mail
to remind the dog and grand-kids
that he was only on vacation.

Hank Greene

I BECAME AN ART CRITIC

In the museum that afternoon
The tour guide lead us from
Painting to painting
Extolling the myriad virtues of
The Modern Painters.

We stopped in front of a painting with many
Squares, triangles and circles:
Notice the ambivalence between
Surface and depth.
See how the images create
Speed and spontaneity.
How well the artist has reached
The ideal abstract solution!

We lingered in front of a huge canvas,
All red,
With two white dots:
What implicit meanings are contained within the
Structured surface!
How the canvas bulges with
Implied volume!
What infinite subtlety, sophistication and richness
Of color!
What achievement of expression through reduction
Of form!

At home that evening my wife greeted me by
Proudly displaying
A multi-colored finger painting
Smeared on a newspaper by our six-year old.

I stood transfixed,
Then chanted:
He painted not the things he saw
But the feelings they aroused
Within him.
The painting is his important moment
Which captured a sense of
Infinite solitude.
This is a remarkable example of
Intuitive spacing
Of the whole picture area.
His colors evoke associations
Beyond the reach of words.

She lead me to a chair,
Stroked my brow
And dialed the doctor.

Harold Leland Johnson

WORDS OF A FEATHER

I round up my ducks
my geese
my swans
three each
put them in postal cages
and ship them to the Poetry Contest.

I wait.

The Judges put on their crinoline glasses
sit up on their embroidered pillows
and grimly signal the postman in.

But the first goose hisses and flares.
the first Judge
scores it
obviously an anapest
and shooes it out.

The swan
has a bad iambic foot
from being jerked out of the crate.
It bleeds a little on the Judge's white glove.
The contest chairman
hurriedly stuffs it
into the proper self-addressed stamped envelope.

Finally, the Judges all smile.
The ducks are passing in review.
Then the head duck plops a few four-letter words
and the rest follow suit.

So I get them all back, keep the useful parts
for a fricasee
and bang the lid on the garbage can.

Right now,
I'm fattening up a few poems
for the Poultry Contest.

Michael Kase

EXCUSE ME, BUT THIS IS USELESS

Hey Merlin
I can't get that goddamn sword outta that stone!
Man I've tried and I'm tired.
How 'bout some other action—
Like maybe a dagger out of a rock?
Success is rare—
And if I do succeed that stone will be useless,
And right now it makes a great conversation piece.
Listen man, if it's that important,
Put an ad in the Sunday paper
Or give Lancelot a call, he needs the work.
What would I do with that sword anyway?
Hang it over the fireplace?
Stick it in someone's gut?
Melt it into bullion?
Sell it? Trade it?
I don't mean to be nosey,
But I'd like to know what I'm doin'
And why I'm doin' it!
Now don't tell me 'bout Camelot—
You search for it—
I can't spend my whole life dreamin',
And anyway I don't wanna be King
And I don't wanna Kingdom.
I jus' need a couple of horses,
A piece of land, Guinevere
And a red sunset.
No offense intended Merlin,
After all you're a helluva magician.

Patrick Kelly

THREE STOOGES IN GEORGIA

There were three of us. We spent the aestivating months
in a darkened theatre; ourselves packed together before
a silver screen bigger than our Aunt's bed sheets. There
to solidify our opinions concerning the intimate nature
of Man. (Is Art a reflection of Reality, or, is Reality a
reflection of Art?)

O, it was Moe! And it was Shemp! And Curly! Or
Larry! Somehow escaped from the Borscht Belt
and come down South on celluloid with their weird
haircuts and as weird accents—loud! boisterous! Un-
couth! Stupid, yet moneyed. We never understood how
Yankees like the Three Stooges could live without gain-
ful employment. We yearned to go North and talk and
act like them. Freedom!

We wanted to run buzz saws across our friend's head;
put his pinkie in a pencil sharpener; back over him with
a moving van at high speeds. We wanted to cut a rusty
after the movie Saturday and spend all day Sunday re-
cuperating from being poked in the eye; bopped on the
head; and recovering from unsuspected uppercuts!

The seat of Moe's trousers looked as if a family of share-
croppers had moved out. Larry's didn't fare much better.
Shark-skin trousers and white socks and brown shoes!
(although the films were in b & w, we knew just how
they dressed—we spent a Winter in Tampa and saw a
whole assload of Northerners dressed that way. However, they were strangely silent and did not run buzz
saws over their friends' heads. They didn't do anything
except sit around and look up and down the streets and
complain about Florida.)

O, there was Leon Erroll. Edgar Kennedy and his famous slow burn. Ollie Hardy from Savannah and Stan Laurel from London. But these others of the shark-skin trousers and Yiddish humor? We yearned to go North and talk and act like them.

So we spent the torpid summer in the picture show.

We went home Saturday and tried out the jokes. Wham! Bop! Booooooing! Blat!

The power saw we ran across our friend's head cut deep and its own shrill whine was drowned out by his horror show scream.

The joke was on us. We ran.

Sunday we went to his funeral. Monday we went to juvenile detention.

The Stooges in their very first short for Columbia Pictures, *Woman Haters,* 1934, with Marjorie White.

Roger W. Langton

DUMPING HUMPTY

humpty dumpty shat
(a contraction of shit
and sat similar to stroft)
on the wall
the king was upset
and sent moe and two
petty bureaucratic friends
called the king's men
in charge of sanitation
(sanitary engineers)
to clean it up
h. d. was startled
by their official
presence and
being reprimanded
fell off the wall
larry one of the petty
bureaucrats suggested
that they forget
the shit and
try to put h.d. back
together
if not again then for
the first time
so moe sewed the left leg
to the right arm pit
while curly the other
petty bureaucrat tried to
make sense of the head
the front was pasted
on the back and soon
h. d. could see in all
directions

about that time a brick
loosened by h. d's fall
fell on larry's head who
then blamed moe and the
scene went wild
bricks flying in all
directions and when it
undid the wall and settled
poor h. d. was buried alive
although wounded
while the shit was everywhere
so they reported to the king
that the mission was
accomplished

Ronald Koertge

THE SIGN SAID

LIVE   NUDE   PSYCHEDELIC   DANCER

friday & saturday

So I dropped in on Sunday, Monday,
Tuesday, Wednesday and Thursday

hoping I was reading my implications
right and they'd have a

DEAD   NUDE   PSYCHEDELIC   DANCER

but

except for the girl behind the bar
who looked like she had one foot
in the grave

there was nothing going on.

Gary E. Ligi

I'M DYING

I'm dying and this lady is asking me
for sausage. "I need
a quarter pound of sweet," she says.
"and half a pound of hot."

her son, I guess it's her son,
keeps fingering the ricotta
in the cooler. he's already picked his nose
and rubbed his finger on the glass.
I think she feeds him only eggs
he smells so bad. he keeps on screaming:
"mama, mama, come look
at the funny man."

"I'm dying," I tell her.
"the weather's been pretty hot,"
she says. the line has stretched around
the shop and clear around the corner. "hmmm,"
she keeps saying, "hmmm" and "hmmm."

a cop shoots a black man
carrying two cases of dog food
and a portable radio
through a broken window across the street.

I hear the boy squeal as an old man
tries to twist his ear off.
others say: "did you see that?
"did you see that?

I cough and when I do
the blood begins to spill
from my lips. "I'm dying," I say
and get the lady's sausage.
"oh, give me half a pound of cheese."
the man with her son's ear between his fingers says
"listen, bag, the poor kid's dying
and ain't none of us got all day."

Gerald Locklin

FRATERNAL LOYALTIES

When the owner unjustly sacked
his two best bartenders,
I vowed I would never again darken his doorway.

It's been three months now,
and I haven't been back

and I hear that the fired bartenders
are in there living it up five nights a week.

WEIGHT WATCHERS

When my stomach was so bad
that I kept throwing up
and lost ten pounds,

people were stopping me to remark,
"Gerry, you look great?
What are you, on some kind of
a health kick or something?"

Gerald Locklin

ONE OF THE MANY WHO ARE HELPING TO PAY FOR THE MGM GRAND HOTEL

This middle-aged gentleman
is neither stupid nor a drunk,

still he sat in the bar and repeated,
"Counter, hah! What good does it do
to count the deck? Aren't the cards
just as good for the dealer
as they are for the player?"

When I pointed out that the dealer
has options and gets to the deck first,

he repeated, "It's the same deck
for the dealer and the player."

So I said, "Suppose you're holding twelve
and you know that there are nothing but
face cards left in the deck?
Is that an advantage?"

He shifted his stance: "If they catch on you're counting
they'll shuffle the deck anyway."

"Why do they do that," I asked,
"if counting isn't an advantage."

"It's the same deck for everyone," he said.

I began to feel like a character
in a Robert Frost dialogue.

The Stooges try to fool Bud Jamison in *Healthy, Wealthy and Dumb*, 1938.

James Magorian

THE NIGHT SHIFT AT THE POETRY FACTORY

The older poets are showing the new ones
around, getting their identification
badges pinned on at the proper angle,
showing them where the cafeteria
and rest rooms are located (the short
cuts and hiding places come later).

A gray-haired laureate has a metaphor locked
in a vise and is filing off rough edges.

The foreman distributes book reviews
and then snaps a prize-money whip
over the workers' heads.

A sonneteer is at the tool cage
checking out a rhyme.

"Stay on the other side
of the yellow safety lines,"
warns a cautious editor.

The grinders are run only by imagists,
and they have a special union.

A ballad-maker comes in late
with his black lunch box under
his arm and begins to sweep
broken voices out of the aisles.

"I'm only working here until I can get
enough money to be somebody else,"
mutters the epigrammatist-in-residence.

The welders are the most admired:
silent in their dark heavy masks
they put together narrative poems
and their brilliance explodes
from behind high screens.

"Is it true that the scabs get all
the foundation grants?" asks
a visiting anthologist.

The oily iron bins of scrap poems
and odds and ends of punctuation
are towed away by small tractors.

Everyone in the free verse department
just got a promotion.

"The conveyor belt broke on Assembly Line 4
and a lot of good adjectives were lost,"
sighs an inventory control inspector.

Resting under an electric sunrise,
the poets wait for the quitting bell
and think back on all the poems
they have made; outside the factory
the pale moon hangs haughtily
in the morning sky like
a cosmic rejection slip.

MATH PROBLEM

Alphonse, Herman, and Bertha
have 17 apples to divide
among themselves. Alphonse
and Bertha are on train A
approaching point X at 83 mph.
Herman is on train B approaching
point X at 70 mph. How old is Bertha?

Robert Matte Jr.

CAKES FOR ALL OCCASIONS

A baker
his specialty was
"Cakes For All Occasions."

He had progressed far beyond
the toy soldiers, race cars, cowboys,
and wedding figures which decorated
the tops of most cakes.

For a client celebrating a divorce
he provided a cake which showed
a couple in bed with an angry
husband looking on.

A cake for a dog's birthday party
was crowned with six beagles
lifting their legs against a
giant fire hydrant.

The grand opening of a tattoo parlor
resulted in a cake with patriotic
overtones. A drunken sailor was
shown having his derriere prermanently
inscribed with the American flag.

His all time favorite was a cake
ordered for a terminally ill patient.
On it sat St. Peter next to the pearly
gates. In his hand was a little sign
which read: "See You Soon!"

Ann Menebroker

SERIES 4

well! you tall old shit!
i am after your ass,
not your soul!

when you are in the mood,
i'm not.
when i am in the mood,
you're not.

and the times we have both
been for it,
the doorbell rings,

or someone who is used to our
ways, walks in
without wondering
if anything ever goes on here
besides the lights.

Robert Murphy

I USE TO DRIVE A CAB

in new york city for money
a hell of a fistful
apes in tennis shoes at kennedy
going to flushing
during the world fair
                        nobody invited me
shit I thought they were all
out of towners anyways
maybe coming all the way from newark
through the tubes
                    my son got expelled
refusing to drink
his urine
            a great believer in health
my wife worked as a nursing aid
                            got mugged
and the two cops
                lost
twenty minutes of coffee break
                            my friend
six months in the hospital
closing his side
growing a wider nose
trying to stop his left eye watering
he has a spasm
                he showed me the scar
no water only blood
half an inch under his tit
and I said
            jeeze we gotta move
the fuck outta here
                    mid-december
cold as a bastard
                    in a rented truck

this old windy farmhouse
the snow never melted
                          till may
of that first year
my daughter crying
                              cause God lived outside
and probably froze to death
                            on welfare
put me to work
polishing brass in the state office complex
emptying paint buckets
washing venetian blinds
                         foodstamps
and free hot lunches
for the kids in school
and I said we gotta get the fuck
                            outta here
started writing poems
                    nobody
understood
               everybody rejected and I lost
stamps envelopes typewriter ribbons
and a desk full of reduced subscription rates
even prison poets get published
in this free economy editors told me
they were only accepting
paterson poems by professional poets
or if I could get walt
to sign my draft card
                  with permission to publish

Opal L. Nations

CONDUCT TO AVOID
AT THE BALL

Lady should not enter or glide across hall unattended.
No gent at balls should enter ladies' dressing room.
Never lead lady into hall by hand, always produce arm.
Do not arrange next dance when current is in progress.
Gent must wait until music strikes to select lady.
Gent should not keep lady on foot for next dance
    when wishing to sit.
Gent should not leap upon vacant seat next to lady
    if stranger.
Gent should not press bare hand to lady's waist during
    waltz if without glove or pocket linen.
Ladies never select large gents to hold flowers, fans
    or gloves during dance unless husband or relative.
Gents should not entwine waist of lady until music
    strikes, hands and arms to drop limp when
    music stops.
Gent should never bury lady's face in cloud of
    tobacco smoke on dance floor.
Never eat supper in gloves, white kids are used during
    dancing.
Gents must keep keen eye on ladies during evening
    to prevent them sitting it out the night long.
No gent must play clown in ball hall; breakdowns and
    unusual sounds should not occur, as with
    swaggering and tossing the arms about.
Lady is not obliged to let Gent into own house after
    ball, but can register requests for next day.
Do not make display of leaving ball through veranda
    windows.
Ladies must never engage two gents for the same
    ball even if lady is cumbersome, excepting the
    waltz where a sharing of work is agreed prior
    to it.

Members of hosts' family should not dance frequently
    unless substitutes are sought out.
Do not convey long whispered conversation into
    others' ears during ball.
Also avoid loud hearty talk and romping beneath
    tables.
Conduct, dress and deportment should not be such
    as to draw large knots of guests.
Gent should not remove lady's coiffure when refused
    an invitation.
Do not sweep across ball room upon partner's feet.
Do not select partner far less in height when dancing
    Sailor's Hornpipe.
Do not suck earrings of lady during performance of
    last waltz.
Do not enquire into lady's cleavage when gaze is
    averted.
Avoid long lasting fingerprints upon lady partner's
    rear.
Do not waylay couples with toe of shoe when
    whisking by.
Do not loosen garments of partner when sailing through
    darkened corners of hall.
Do not puff cigarette when dancing and stub out
    same upon waiter's tray.
Never steer lady from floor onto balcony during
    slow waltz to look at stars.

A scene from *Squareheads of the Round Table,* 1948, with Jacques O'Mahoney.

Kent Nussey

STOOGIST CRUSADE

The Grail
is three baggy short men
with imbecile energies
and cinematic eyes
"Find them!" said the Merlin
of my slapstick sleep
"Find them, and
you'll find
the Dream."

Kent Nussey

SHEMP'S BLUES

Third-man themes have always
whistled through my pounded brains
crow-barred and ice-picked
bopped with
the bottoms of hard little hands
they called me imposter
preferred faceless fat men
to my suffering jowls.
I endured like a Christian
praying the rewards of my pain
might be stored like clear film
in round, shiny tins
opened at the Judgement
for the saints to see
and I, limp-haired and crow-eyed
will be redeemed
the Trinity
complete.

Kent Nussey

MOE HOWARD DIES AT SEVENTY-EIGHT

Last time I saw him, in
a small room on the seventh floor
of the Hemenway Hotel
a scuffling behind doors
laden with locks and heavy paranoias
opened to bare walls, one mirror
and closet. An open Bible on his bed.
Hermit of the wind
he stole crumbs from the pigeons
gave his last ten to some needy Indians
finished his dialogue on objective reality
with an expletive hurled like a pie
at the eye of God
snarled and snapped
"Back off porcupine!"
and satisfied he'd been heard
allowed himself to drift into newsprint
like a poem
lapsing into prayer.

Kirk Robertson

TENNIS ANYONE?

the first marriage license
issued in missoula county
was returned
unused
the TV says.

the bartender's talking
to a young blonde tennis type
at the far end
of the bar.

i ask for a beer.

he comes over
fills the glass & whispers
not bad, eh?
she wants me to come
over & fix her motorcycle.
oh yeah?
i think i can manage to
do that he says winking.

but she's now on her way out
the door with some
jimmy connors type.

shit the bartender says
there must be a more romantic
job than managing a beer bar
maybe i can get on down
at S & M sporting goods.

up on the TV back of the bar
marlboro men in 4 wheel drives
ride off with all the girls.

David Shevin

LOSING FACE

I started missing pieces about a month ago. Madge and I went
shopping all afternoon, and when we got back to the car she
said My GOD your cheek is missing. I said that I must have
left it on the table at the hairdresser's, but Pierre hadn't seen
it. So I combed the hair over the empty spot for a few days.
Then we were over for dinner at the Finkles' and my nose fell
right into the soup. My jaw just *dropped* to see it there, but I
still had control over that. At home, Ward tried to steam it
back on. That just evaporated it, though. The skin made a
mess and the nostril hairs were all over the light bulb. About
that time little Debbie took both my ears in to school, because
she wanted to hear the teacher better. Wouldn't you know it
—she came back without them. Said they got taken away at
lunch time. I started to give her what for, but Ward said to
shut my mouth and when I did I swallowed it. When I got
over that, I decided to just turn the other cheek which got it
all twisted and ugly. Dr. Proctor gave me these lovely pros-
thetic cheeks—you can hardly tell that the others are missing.
He's going to start work on the mouth on the eleventh. In the
meantime, a week passed and I went out on Saturday afternoon to get Debbie for dinner and there she was with the
neighbor boy, Faron Trembling, playing a card game on the
lawn. They both—I swear to God—had their pants off. Well,
my eyes just popped right out of my head. We carried them
inside and I laid down until Ward came home. He'd been over
at Max Finkle's at their weekly game and was grumbling and
cussing. I asked what the matter was. He said he lost his *ass*
at poker. That was two days ago and he's getting meaner than
a bear. Which is why I'm locked in the guest room and I'm
not coming out until he finds it.

Leon Spiro

THE THREE STOOGES PLUS DAVID FROST

And it came about, dash,
Holy Moe roared down from a'top The Mount,
"Richard Nixon—Thou Forgot My 10 Laws!"

Then Larry, the Lesser Saint
Came in a dream to Jerry Ford, saying:
"Pardon, Pardon, Pardon, I'm His Pie in The Sky,
All over your Unelected Face,
Incumbent, BAH!"

And Curly, The Jesus One, combed His Beard,
Thus saying: "Beau Carter, practice what I preach,
Your baptism's yet to come, even as
I Shall Reappear!"

Then Shemp, the foreign fourth Frosty stooge,
Taking Curly's Place, simply sighed,
Hitching Jimmy Carter by the pants
To his favorite star.

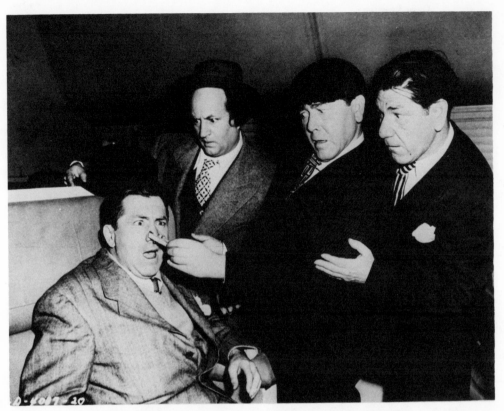

Curly (complete with clothespin and hair) makes a cameo appearance
with Larry, Moe and Shemp in *Hold That Lion,* 1947.

Gary Sterling

AN AH AWLSO SLEEUPS ON BUNAYHNUHZ

Ahm de Stoog
Ahm de Stoog
An Ah wauk aroun
Wid mah feets on de groun
An Ah looks at de skies
An gets pies in mah eies

Shemp gets a taste of his favorite pie in *Heavenly Daze,* 1948.

Seth Wade

COULD'VE BEEN MY EYE

something-i-ate
& so back &
forth chasing it
around saturday morning

over the egg salad
in back of the strudel
& back

thru the potroast & potatoes
& what-is-your-thumb-doing-in-my-mouth

John Stevens Wade

HOUSE GUESTS

Should have been out
instead of in.
Nothing to do
but be what they
must think I am:
glad all over
to have them here.
So I shake hands
and say to them:
how long it's been!
And yes, since I
insist, they'll stay
all night. Next day
I wait for them
to leave, but they
make plans. Why yes,
how good it is,
and so much fun!
Then all week long
they talk and eat.
I hide my hands,
but they don't care.
They know how much
I want them here.
From cupboard to
pantry and then
to bed, there is
so much to do
and say I can't
break in. When I
start talking, they
make plans. Kitchen
to bedroom is
how a day ends.

So I ask them
to leave, but they
don't hear. I try
to drag them out,
and all I get
is a handful
of air. When I
go outside, they
lock themselves in.
They don't look up
when I scratch at
windows; they don't
even come to
the door. This is
my house, I keep
shouting at them —
my house! But I'm
beginning to
think I don't live
here any more.

A scene from *Tassels in the Air,* 1938.

Martin Willitts, Jr.

JESSE JAMES TAKES MISS GOODY TWO SHOES
TO A FORMAL DANCE AT HER HIGH SCHOOL
AND MEETS HER PARENTS

Jesse spent 3 hours duding up,
shining his boots and spurs,
putting on his fringe vest,
combing his hair with gasoline.

All this preparation for a date
with Miss Goody Two Shoes,
the gal who stole his foolish heart,
the gal who tries to clean up his act.

They were to go to her High School Formal
to celebrate the championship
losing football team. He'd rather rob banks,
than wear a tux like a tenderfoot.

Her parents greeted him with questions:
How do you make a living?
Do you have honorable intentions?
Will you bring her home before midnight?

He sat in their parlor wiping his palms
on his Wrangler jeans. Then she appeared
looking like a bridal catalogue.
His throat became as dry as the desert.

This was the big moment to settle down,
she looked like his favorite horse.
He asked her the big question:
What are you doing Saturday morning?

Wedding bells rang in her mountainous breasts.
She said yes with a tremble in her knees.
He told her he wanted a partner in crime,
and she hit him in the eye with her fist.

Fred Thaballa

HUCK

In a sunny room out the window a huge pine tree
dressed in jeans and polo shirt and boots
looking out the window the picture of a pose
looking out the window his chin in his hand
looking out the window looking hearing the phone ring
answers: yes
nodding letting that go by seeing possibilities
taking the time for the flow to settle a bit
taking the easy way out letting breath form clouds
letting clouds form smoke letting smoke form
rings around the sun putting the receiver down.

Huck turns to the door opens it enters the hallway
turns left at the kitchen past the kitchen
into the pantry opens the refrigerator opens a beer
walks to window of kitchen: view from window
is wall of next door house: small area between the two.
Cat sits beside plants. Assorted garbage.
Sink of dirty dishes. Lamp shade from the ceiling.

Huck goes through dinette through dining room
through French doors into living room
sits on couch watching TV *The Three Stooges*:
Moe hits Larry hits Curly with hammer.

A scene from *A-Plumbing We Will Go,* 1940.

A.D. Winans

THE GREEN HORNET

sentenced to san quentin
for stabbing kato to death
with a rusty canopener

appears once a year with
the great gildersleeve at

a savings and loan
serving cookies and coffee
and dreaming of the good old days.

TARZAN

was slipped a lethal dose
of spanish fly
raped cheetah
tore jane in half
found him in the trunk
crying between two
spare tires.

THE LONE RANGER

drank himself into
a coma before
he was forty
sits around watching
howard cosell eye
alex karas

voted halloween drag queen
of 76   married
tonto's sister and
was murdered in chinatown by
a half breed.

THE INVISIBLE MAN

Addendum

STOOGISM

i dreamt of
moe
last night
he was
crying
he took the
laughter
out of his
head
and
thanked me
and
when i saw
myself about
to cry
he whispered:
wake up and
go to sleep
and i did

—Paul F. Fericano

"If there's one thing I like better than honey and ketchup, it's baloney and whipped cream—and we don't have any."
—Moe Howard

111